STRATEGY AND TACTICS

AMPHIBIOUS
WARFARE

STRATEGY AND TACTICS

AMPHIBIOUS WARFARE

IAN SPELLER AND CHRISTOPHER TUCK

MBI Publishing Company

This edition first published in 2001 by
MBI Publishing Company,
Galtier Plaza, Suite 200
175 East Fifth Street
St Paul, MN 55101 USA
www.motorbooks.com

The information in this book is true and complete to the best of our
knowledge. All recommendations are made without any guarantee on the
part of the author or publisher, who also disclaim any liability incurred in
connection with the use of this data or specific details.

The opinions expressed herein are those of the authors, and do not necessarily
reflect the official policy of the Joint Services Command and Staff College,
or the Ministry of Defence.

We recognize that some words, model names and designations, for example,
mentioned herein are the property of the trademark holder. We use them
for identification purposes only. This is not an official publication.

MBI Publishing Company books are also available at discounts in bulk quantity
for industrial or sales-promotional use. For details write to Special Sales Manager
at Motorbooks International Wholesalers & Distributors, Galtier Plaza, Suite 200,
175 East Fifth Street, St Paul, MN 55101 USA.

Library of Congress Cataloging-in-Publication Data Available.

ISBN 0-7603-1144-7

Editorial and design by
Amber Books Ltd
Bradley's Close
74-77 White Lion Street
London N1 9PF

Project Editor: Naomi Waters
Design: Floyd Sayers
Picture Research: Lisa Wren

*Page 1: US Marines in LCPRs (Landing Craft Personnel, Rubber) off Fort
Pierce, Florida. These rubber boats were used for secret missions and night landings.*

Printed in Italy – Nuova GEP, Cremona

CONTENTS

THE STRATEGIC CONTEXT

The ability to deploy a military force across the seas to a chosen point has often been decisive in determining success in war.

An amphibious operation involves the projection of a military force from the sea onto a hostile, or a potentially hostile, shore. There are four key types of amphibious operation – assault, raid, withdrawal and demonstration – and these are described in detail later. Amphibious operations share many characteristics with other maritime activities, including the administrative disembarkation of forces on a friendly shore and simple ferry activities between ports; indeed, specialist amphibious shipping is frequently employed on tasks like these. However, the need to land military forces on a hostile shore without the asset of traditional port facilities is a defining characteristic and sets amphibious warfare apart from other, less demanding, activities.

LEFT: A light tank is unloaded from a transport ship into a landing craft prior to the US landing at Guadalcanal in the Solomon Islands on 7 August 1942. Operation Watchtower, the assault on Guadalcanal, was the first of many successful American amphibious operations during the Pacific War. The initial landing on 7 August was unopposed. However, fierce fighting ensued inland and the island was not finally secured until February 1943.

ABOVE: This drawing offers an imaginative interpretation of a Danish (Viking) attack on the English coast. The sacking of the monastery of Lindisfarne in Northumbria in 793 AD marked the beginning of Viking attacks on the British Isles and these were to continue until the 11th century. The Vikings also attacked the coast of mainland Europe, establishing settlements in places such as Normandy in France.

The ability to conduct successful amphibious operations has been a vital factor in warfare since ancient times. Over two-thirds of the earth's surface is ocean, and a maritime force's ability to exploit its access to land has been of profound strategic significance. With strength at sea, a maritime power can strike an opponent's coast at whatever time and place they choose. When this factor is linked to the ability to land a balanced military force, the results have often been devastating.

Amphibious forces offer secure, independent, forward-deployed operating bases. They can be configured to conduct a range of operations, from humanitarian support following a natural disaster, to high-intensity war fighting against sophisticated opposition. The strategic reach and mobility provided by maritime assets means that amphibious forces can deploy or withdraw, and concentrate or disperse, at will, without the need to negotiate over-flight or basing facilities. They therefore have political independence and military flexibility. Amphibious forces can exploit the element of surprise, hitting the enemy when they least expect it, and where they are least prepared. They can sail early in times of crisis, either in a blaze of publicity to demonstrate resolve and capability, or covertly when a more diplomatic approach is required. Once in theatre, an amphibious force can be held in international waters, offering presence without occupation, and leverage without embroilment. If embarked in appropriate shipping, an amphibious force can be maintained at sea almost indefinitely or, if necessary, can be sustained ashore in protracted conflict. In sum, the independence, mobility, flexibility and sustainability of a balanced amphibious task force, particularly when supported by suitable naval vessels and furnished with air support, make it an extremely capable instrument.

By nature, amphibious operations are challenging. Conducted at the juncture between the military and naval spheres of competence, they have the potential to demonstrate the worst characteristics of both and the best characteristics of neither. Amphibious forces face hazards posed by the force of nature as well as man-made defences. To rapidly build up combat power on the shore before enemy forces counter-attack has always proved to be a difficult task. The simple logistical problem of embarking and disembarking troops, vehicles and equipment without conventional port facilities complicates the planning and conduct of operations. However, despite all of these problems, landing a balanced military force on an enemy shore has been one of the key means of achieving success in conflict throughout history.

AMPHIBIOUS WARFARE IN HISTORY

Amphibious forces have been used to good effect for as long as mankind has ventured onto the sea. Historical evidence shows that as early as 1200 BC the Egyptian Empire was subjected to attacks by seaborne raiders from the Mediterranean islands and the coastline of southern Europe. The Egyptians repulsed most of the raids by these so-called 'Sea Peoples', but some of the invaders established themselves along the coast, such as the Philistines in Palestine. Centuries later, the Greeks made full use of amphibious forces. The defeat of the Athenian expedition to Sicily between 413 and 415 BC stands as a key turning-point in the Peloponnesian War. Later still, the British Isles suffered their first major amphibious invasion in 55 BC when Julius Caesar brought his legions across the Channel. The Romans landed on a beach near present-day Dover, where they faced fierce opposition by the Celtic forces waiting for them on the shore. In an early example of naval fire support, the Roman ships were brought in close so that their catapults could fire down on the defenders.

The Roman invasion was the first of many to hit the British Isles. In the centuries that followed, succeeding waves of Angles, Saxons, Vikings and Normans all sought to conquer Britain from the sea. The Norman invasion of 1066 involved an estimated 20,000 infantry and 12,000 cavalry. The English King Harold's defeat at the Battle of Hastings came only weeks after his army had marched north to successfully repulse a Viking invasion at the Battle of Stamford Bridge. However, proficiency in amphibious operations was not restricted to the European continent. During the 15th century, the Chinese general Cheng Ho led a series of expeditions throughout the Indian Ocean. By the time of his final expedition, which took place in 1433, his combined land and naval force had extracted tribute from most of the nations that were located along the shore of the Indian Ocean.

Historically weak on the land but strong at sea, England (and, from 1707, Britain) made good use of amphibious forces in a series of wars against both Spain and France. Francis Drake's raid on Spanish possession in the Caribbean between 1585 and 1586 was a prelude to a series of successful amphibious operations that included the capture of Gibraltar in 1704, the seizure of Louisbourg in 1758 and of Quebec in 1759, the model landing at Aboukir Bay in 1801 and the burning of Washington in 1814. However, the difficulty of conducting amphibious operations in the age of sail was

BELOW: The Norman conquest of 1066 was the last occasion when England was successfully invaded from the sea. The transport of a balanced military force from across the English Channel was a considerable logistical feat and was the only way in which William of Normandy could militarily support his claim to the English throne.

demonstrated by an equally long list of failures, including Drake's final expedition to the Caribbean in 1595 and the disastrous expedition to Cartagena in 1741 after which, of the 10,000 men who embarked for the operation, only 2600 could be accounted for. British victories against the Spanish Armada in 1588 and at Trafalgar in 1805 thwarted Spanish and French attempts to gain sufficient control of the sea to launch amphibious invasions of the British Isles.

One of the key problems for amphibious forces was that the land and sea elements of the force had to provide mutual support. This was often difficult, as the naval and land force commanders had little understanding of, or sympathy for, the troubles of their sister service. The army's need to maintain contact with the fleet in order to guarantee re-supply and re-embarkation — as well as the difficulty in landing horses for the cavalry and guns for the artillery — often meant that amphibious forces could not gain full advantage from the strategic mobility of their naval transports. The landing of British troops at Aboukir Bay in 1801, despite heavy opposition on the beaches, showed that opposed landings were possible, but, even so, they remained difficult and dangerous.

By the end of the 19th century, these problems were exacerbated by the advent of long-range coastal defence guns, sea mines and torpedo boats. The arrival of submarines in the early part of the 20th century meant that operations close to enemy bases would be much more dangerous than had been the case. At the same time, improvements in land communications and the growth of large, professional armies threatened to erode the strategic advantages of amphibious forces. Armies could now utilize railways and modern roads to rapidly move forces to meet the threat of invasion and therefore small amphibious forces could not rely on meeting weak and poorly coordinated defenders.

The creation of local defence organizations and militias further complicated the matter; the German Chancellor Otto von Bismarck reputedly stated that if the British landed an army on the Prussian coast he would call out the local police force and have it arrested. Improvements in defensive firepower — with the introduction of the machine-gun, the magazine rifle and quick-firing artillery — appeared to make opposed landings at best hazardous, and at worst impossible. As the new century dawned, many people doubted whether amphibious warfare had any future at all.

Contrary to their expectations, amphibious forces became even more relevant in the 20th century. Despite the chastening experience at Gallipoli in 1915, where the Allied landing force incurred heavy losses in the face of determined Turkish defences, techniques and equipment developed rapidly. The Americans and, to a lesser extent, the British, studied the lessons of Gallipoli in the inter-war period and this laid the foundations for their successful amphibious operations in Europe and the Pacific during World War II. Likewise, the Japanese built on their experience of

RIGHT: Horses landing from ships belonging to Henry III in 1269. Special ships were built to transport horses during the Crusades. The transports would beach stern first before ramps were lowered over the stern, down which horses could be led. This 19th-century artist appears to anticipate the development of 20th-century landing craft equipped with doors built into the hull to enable transport to be landed directly onto the beach.

successful operations during the Russo-Japanese War of 1904–5 and employed their forces to good effect during the 1930s and 1940s in their wars against China, the United States and the colonies of France, Britain and the Netherlands. Even traditional land powers such as Germany and the Soviet Union sought to employ amphibious forces, albeit with mixed results.

By 1945 amphibious forces had developed from their humble beginnings to represent a major strategic asset. With new equipment and techniques, amphibious forces could now transport, land and sustain ashore large, balanced armies with the full range of supporting arms. The limitations of previous centuries had been overcome. A bewildering variety of new ships, craft

LEFT: Henry VIII of England embarking in a Royal ship at Dover. Although he increased the size of his navy, Henry also constructed a series of powerful coastal defence forts along the south coast of England in order to protect the realm against attack from the sea. Many of these were concentrated on the coastline opposite Boulogne and Calais, the narrowest part of the Channel.

BELOW: British forces under General Abercromby overcome fierce French resistance on the beach at Aboukir Bay in 1801. In the face of French infantry, artillery and dragoons, the British managed to succeed in that most difficult of all military operations, an opposed landing.

and equipment had been designed that allowed assaulting forces to suppress defences at the beach line and to establish sufficient combat power ashore to seize, hold and expand a viable beachhead. At the same time, the strategic mobility provided by maritime power, as well as the advantage of being able to strike at a time and place of their own choosing, provided amphibious forces with an extremely decisive advantage over their land-based opponents.

Amphibious forces proved just as relevant in the years of troubled peace that followed 1945. The ability to deploy a mobile, self-sufficient and self-sustaining force provided politicians with useful military options. Amphibious forces were deployed to good effect in a series of conflicts and crises, including the Korean War (1950), the Suez Crisis (1956), in the Lebanon (1958), Vietnam (1964–75), the Falkland Islands (1982), Grenada (1983) and during the Gulf War (1990–91). The attributes of mobility and flexibility have proved to be of enduring value. The combination of trained manpower, transport shipping and a mix of landing craft, amphibious vehicles and helicopters means that modern amphibious forces

BELOW: Horses of the 11th Hussars are embarked on board the troopship *Tyrone* at Kingston ready for passage to the east. The embarkation and disembarkation of horses was a difficult and time-consuming process.

are valuable tools for supporting humanitarian operations and in disaster relief. However, the key feature of all amphibious forces remains their ability to conduct that most exacting of military operations: an amphibious assault.

ASSAULTS

There are four key types of amphibious operation: assaults; raids; withdrawals; and demonstrations.

The amphibious assault is the principal type of amphibious operation and provides the main focus for this book. Amphibious assaults are conducted in order to establish a landing force on a hostile shore so that one of three objectives may be achieved.

One of these objectives is to conduct further combat operations inland. Examples of this include the North African landings of November 1942, the landings in Sicily in 1943 and at Salerno in 1943 and the Normandy landings in June 1944. In these cases, the amphibious operation was the prelude to a major land campaign. This has been described as a 'theatre entry' role.

Another possible objective is to obtain a site for an advanced naval or air base. The

majority of the landings conducted by both Japan and the United States in the Central Pacific during World War II fall into this category. For example, the main reason behind the US assault on Iwo Jima in February 1945 was that the area could be a valuable forward airbase in support of the strategic bombing campaign against Japan.

Denying the use of an area or facilities to the enemy is another possible objective of an amphibious assault. Operation Ironclad, the British assault on Vichy French-held Madagascar in 1942, was an example of this type of operation, and was designed to prevent Japanese use of the Diego Suarez naval base.

The landings can be conducted against a hostile (defended) shore, as at Gallipoli in 1915 and Tarawa in 1943, or against a potentially hostile shore. In the latter case, the operation is undertaken on the basis that the landing site may become hostile before the operation is completed; a good example of this is the German landings in Norway in 1940. It is obviously better to

land where enemy forces are weak rather than where they are strong; however, completely unopposed landings can rarely be counted upon. Even where the beach itself is not defended by enemy troops – as with the amphibious assault at San Carlos Water during the 1982 Falklands conflict – the landing may be opposed by enemy airforces, naval forces

ABOVE: During the American Civil War, both sides employed spar torpedo boats to attack enemy shipping.

BELOW: Troops of the 9th US Infantry embark in Florida, bound for Cuba in 1898.

ABOVE: Rocket-firing landing ships engage Japanese defences during the US invasion of Leyte in October 1944. For an opposed landing to succeed, enemy defences must be either destroyed or suppressed. To achieve this, a wide variety of specialist ships and craft was developed by the Allies in World War II.

or indirect artillery fire. In the modern world, the potential deployment of mines at sea, in the surf zone and on the beach, and the existence of long-range ballistic missiles equipped with biological, chemical and even nuclear weapons means that even an apparently benign landing site can hold hidden dangers.

The key feature that defines the nature of an amphibious assault is the objective it is designed to achieve. Not all operations fall into the classification given above. During World War II, the Soviet Union developed a unique approach to amphibious operations. Primarily concerned with the land war against Nazi Germany, the Soviets employed amphibious forces to good effect on the flanks and in the rear of advancing or retreating enemy forces. This style of operation, called a desant, reflected the Soviet emphasis on deploying forces in the enemy rear in order to disrupt their cohesion and stability. Amphibious forces were just one means of achieving this effect; other means included parachute drops or tanks exploiting through a gap

in the enemy line. In all cases, the mission was designed to directly support the Soviet land campaign. This particular approach to amphibious warfare was significantly different to that of the United States or United Kingdom.

Between 1941 and 1945 the Soviet Union conducted a total of 110 small 'tactical' amphibious landings and four larger 'operational' type assaults. All of these operations were short range, conducted only a few miles behind the front line ashore. Amphibious forces exploited the enemy coastline in order to achieve a flanking hook, linking up with advancing land forces within 24 hours of the assault, thus reducing the need to maintain the beachhead for an extended period. Supporting the land campaign meant that landings were frequently planned at very short notice; it was not unheard of for the planning and preparation time for small-scale operations to be as little as 24 hours.

Soviet amphibious forces operated in a high-threat environment close to the main body of the enemy. The proximity to the front line meant that many operations could be supported by land-based artillery. The Soviets were also aware of the value of naval gunfire support and tried to suppress enemy defences with heavy fire whenever possible. However, the frequent lack of sufficient support fire led them to place great emphasis on the element of surprise. This was particularly important, as the lack of specialist amphibious shipping meant that Soviet forces relied on existing vessels adapted to this role, which reduced the size and scale of the assaulting force and slowed down the initial assault and build-up. Initially, conventional infantry were employed in the assault and these often received minimal training. Later on in the war, Naval Infantry units trained in amphibious operations were used to spearhead the landings.

Overall, the Soviet Union made good use of amphibious forces during World War II, despite lack of experience in amphibious warfare and the lack of specialist equipment. Concentrating on supporting the land campaign – and thus the need to conduct operations at short notice – brought a unique approach to amphibious operations, one which emphasized speed, surprise, improvisation and flexibility. Although they never achieved the same kind of capability or skill that was demonstrated by the Western Allies, the Soviets demonstrated the gains that even traditional land powers could make by exploiting the potential of amphibious warfare.

RAIDS

Another type of amphibious operation is the amphibious raid. This differs from the conventional amphibious assault in that it includes the pre-planned re-embarkation of the landing force. The objective is occupied for a limited time period, enough to allow the force to achieve their mission. As such, the amphibious raid is limited in time and space and therefore tends to require fewer resources than a conventional assault. Historically the majority of raids have been small in scale, involving at most only a few hundred well-trained soldiers or marines. However, some have been on a larger scale, the most notable of these being the Allied raid on Dieppe in 1942 which was conducted by an entire division, supported by almost 60 tanks and reinforced by three commando units. The failure of this operation, and the heavy losses incurred, highlighted the difficulty of conducting raiding operations on such a large scale.

Raids are conducted for a number of reasons. One of these reasons is to inflict loss or damage on the enemy. An example of this was the British raid on Zeebrugge on 23 April 1918, which attempted to sink blockships in the harbour and deny its use to German submarines. In World

BELOW: Modern amphibious operations require careful planning and preparation. Here US landing craft conduct a training exercise in March 1945 shortly before the landings at Okinawa later that month. The ship in the centre of the picture is the destroyer USS *Morris*.

War II there were many examples of this type of raid, and the British raised special commando units precisely for this reason. A classic example of a commando operation was the raid on the German-occupied Lofoten Islands off northern Norway. In the early hours of the morning on 4 March 1941, 500 men from No.3 and No.4 Commandos stormed ashore. Facing limited opposition, they destroyed 11 factories, set alight 800,000 gallons of oil, sank five German ships and took 225 prisoners, withdrawing to safety before German reinforcements could arrive. Later in the year, on 26 December, the British conducted a second raid on the Lofoten Islands which acted as a diversion for a larger raid conducted against the Norwegian island of Vaagso.

Perhaps the most unusual amphibious raid of the war which was designed to inflict loss or damage on the enemy occurred at the port of St Nazaire in France on 28 March 1942. The Allies were keen to destroy the main dock facility there, which aerial bombing had failed to achieve, as it was the only dry dock on the French Atlantic coast large enough to accommodate the German battleship *Tirpitz*. As a consequence, an old US lend-lease destroyer, HMS *Cambeltown* – disguised as a German vessel in order to bluff its way into the defended harbour – and 16 wooden motor launches carried 600 sailors and commandos, penetrating the Loire estuary under cover of darkness and trying to enter the harbour. Although the Germans saw through the disguise and rained fire down on the vulnerable amphibious force, the landing force was disembarked to create havoc ashore. HMS *Cambeltown* rammed the giant dock-gates and bedded into them. At 1030 hours on the following day, timed

BELOW: British landing craft, mechanized (LCM), lie alongside a transport ship off Dieppe during the raid on that town in August 1942. The raid on Dieppe was a costly failure. The main landing, conducted by the 2nd Canadian Division, achieved none of its objectives and suffered heavy casualties at the hands of the Germans.

LEFT: A damaged Argentine aircraft on Pebble Island after the raid by British special forces on 14 May 1982. The raid demonstrated the potential for small groups of highly trained men to inflict significant damage on important enemy targets. These aircraft could have inflicted heavy casualties on British troops who were landing at San Carlos.

explosives in its bows detonated, killing a large number of curious Germans who had gathered to examine the wreck, and rendering the gates inoperable for the rest of the war. However, this was success at a price. As St Nazaire was heavily defended, few of the raiders were able to re-embark and escape back to Britain. Of the 17 vessels that entered the harbour, only three made it back to Britain, leaving behind them a total of 169 raiders dead and 200 captured.

A more recent example of an amphibious raid designed to inflict loss or damage on the enemy was the British Special Air Service's (SAS) attack on Pebble Island off West Falkland on 14 May 1982. Following the invasion of April 1982, Argentine forces had stationed a number of aircraft on the air strip there. The British commanders were keen to neutralize these aircraft before conducting the main assault landing at San Carlos Water, so 45 men of D Squadron SAS were landed on Pebble Island at night by helicopter and, supported by naval gunfire, they destroyed 11 Argentine ground attack aircraft using demolition charges. They repulsed a half-hearted Argentine counter-attack before successfully withdrawing to the aircraft carrier HMS *Hermes* without loss to themselves.

An amphibious raid may be conducted in order to secure information. This takes the form either of intelligence gathered from prisoners and captured documents or of covert reconnaissance, possibly prior to a full-scale assault. Submarines are often used to transport special forces

offshore, where they can either swim or paddle ashore in canoes or inflatable boats. Today special forces have an array of underwater delivery vehicles that provide covert access to the shore. The successful employment of submarines in this role during World War II, such as HMS *Seraph*, led the US Navy to construct specially designed transport submarines for raiding operations after 1945. The most famous of these, USS *Perch*, participated in numerous covert raids during the Korean War and operated with distinction during the conflict in Vietnam. Operations typically involved the landing of reconnaissance teams, frequently in preparation for an amphibious assault. In August 1966 the *Perch* gained the distinction of being the last US submarine to fire its deck gun in combat, using its two 1.5in (40mm) guns to fire at Viet Cong positions ashore. Later transport submarines, in common with other US submarines, were not fitted with deck guns.

Another reason for carrying out an amphibious raid is to create a diversion. This can occur at the tactical level, as with the diversionary raid conducted by a mixed American and British force at Kunsan in 1950. The aim of this raid was to confuse the North Korean defenders as to the site of the main assault, which was actually taking place at Inchon. Equally, raiding can have the wider strategic aim of forcing an opponent to divert troops away from the main theatre of operations in order to defend a vulnerable coastline. This was a key reason for Allied raiding activities in

ABOVE: US shipping lies at anchor in Wonsan harbour in October 1950. The serious delay to the planned landings, caused by widespread enemy mines, illustrates the requirement for a proper balance of assets in the maritime force – including sufficient mine counter-measures vessels.

World War II. By 1944 Allied raids, and the possibility that they could be followed by major landings, forced the Germans to station 18 divisions in Norway. These divisions could make no contribution to the war effort in either Russia or Italy, nor were they available to defend France against invasion.

Amphibious raids are also carried out to capture individuals or equipment. This can be very important and is frequently a task for special forces. Amphibious forces offer a unique advantage in this kind of operation as, unlike air attacks which can only destroy equipment, they are able to seize equipment or individuals for interrogation or examination. A good example of this kind of operation was the raid on Bruneval in February 1942, conducted in order to seize secret German radar equipment and bring it back to Britain for evaluation. About 100 men were parachuted into France, then advanced to the cliff-top site of the radar station before overwhelming the

defenders and seizing the requisite equipment. Having done this, they clambered down the cliffs to the beach where amphibious landing craft re-embarked them and carried them home. After the war, General Student, who commanded German airborne forces, acknowledged that this raid was a fine example of the cooperation of airborne and amphibious forces.

WITHDRAWALS

A quite different type of amphibious operation is the amphibious withdrawal. Withdrawals involve the re-embarkation of military or civilian personnel and equipment. They may be pre-planned military operations or may involve an emergency embarkation from a hostile, or potentially hostile, shore. Military forces may conduct a withdrawal either as the final stage of an amphibious raid or in order to conduct further amphibious operations elsewhere. If this is the case, the need to tactically reload and

reconfigure the landing force can seriously complicate the process of embarkation. The withdrawal of a military force in contact with the enemy has occurred on numerous occasions, notably at Gallipoli (1916), Dunkirk (1940), Crete (1941) and Korea (1950). In these circumstances, an amphibious withdrawal was the only way to evacuate these forces from a high-threat environment and bring them successfully to a place of safety.

Amphibious forces have frequently been called upon to help evacuate civilian personnel. Amphibious forces have proven to be a valuable asset in what are called Non-Combatant Evacuation Operations (NEOs). The final withdrawal of US citizens from Saigon in 1975 was possible only because helicopters could be flown to and from US shipping held offshore. Likewise, in 1998 British Royal Marines were deployed to the Congo with their landing craft in case they were required to evacuate civilians from

Kinshasa in war-torn Zaire across the River Congo to safety in Brazzaville. Amphibious withdrawals can be a useful tool in both war and peace; their conduct will be examined in greater detail in Chapter Seven of this book.

DEMONSTRATIONS OF STRENGTH AND INTENT

The final type of amphibious operation is the amphibious demonstration, designed either to deceive an enemy or as a show of strength. In a sense, any peacetime exercise falls into the latter category, as it demonstrates the strength of a national capability and can deter a would-be aggressor. Demonstrations in wartime are usually designed to tie down enemy forces or to divert them away from the main area of operations. In order to achieve this, they must appear to pose a credible threat to the force ashore. They may be conducted independently, or as an integral part of an amphibious plan. For example, at Gallipoli, in order to confuse

ABOVE: US Navy LSTs beached at Wonsan with their bow doors open. In the foreground is a USMC tank and a number of amphibious vehicles (LVTs). The LST could embark tanks, vehicles, artillery and heavy supplies and land them through its bow doors directly onto the beach. It provided the backbone of all Allied landings between 1943 and 1945.

the enemy and to divert defending troops away from the main landing beaches to the south, the Allied amphibious landing included a diversion to the north by the Royal Naval Division. Amphibious forces also conducted numerous diversionary operations during the Korean War. For example, in October 1952 a potential landing site behind enemy lines at Kojo was subjected to a preliminary bombardment by US warships. A US Regimental Combat Team then embarked in landing craft and advanced within 5000yds (4572m) of the shore before turning away, demonstrating the US capability in this field. Intelligence reports indicated that, in the months afterwards, the Communists relocated reserve divisions to meet this perceived threat. In this case, the diversion's value was reinforced by a previous demonstration of the amphibious force's potential at Inchon in September 1950.

Perhaps the best example of a successful amphibious demonstration was that of the US Marine Corps and the US Navy during the 1991 Gulf War. A total of 31 amphibious ships carrying 17,000 Marines were deployed to the Gulf. The force at sea included 39 tanks, 112 amphibious assault vehicles, 30 light armoured vehicles and 52 howitzers. This force was configured for a landing operation and conducted numerous rehearsals to ensure that Saddam Hussein got the message. As a result, the Iraqi

defenders were convinced that a major amphibious landing would be directed against the coast of Kuwait, and so to meet it they built beach defences on the vulnerable coastline and diverted five divisions to its defence. This drew forces away from the intended area of Coalition operations and facilitated the armoured left hook through the desert. Without having to land on the mainland of Kuwait, US amphibious forces had neutralized a force roughly 15 times larger than itself. There has rarely been a better example of the value of an amphibious force.

CONCLUSION

Amphibious forces have demonstrated their usefulness in a variety of situations throughout the 20th century. They can be configured to deal with situations right across the spectrum of conflict, from humanitarian and peace-support operations, to low-intensity conflict or high-intensity operations requiring sustained and overwhelming combat power. This book will examine the strategy and tactics of amphibious operations. It will take a thematic approach, analysing each stage of the assault and providing evidence and illustrations from actual operations. The book will demonstrate the problems and pitfalls – as well as the opportunities – presented by amphibious operations in the past, present and future.

FAR RIGHT, TOP: Evacuated South Vietnamese airforce personnel and their families arrive aboard the USS *Blue Ridge* on 29 April 1975. Fifteen South Vietnamese aircraft landed on the *Blue Ridge* that day.

FAR RIGHT, BOTTOM: The USS *Iwo Jima* in the Gulf during the war in 1991. US amphibious capability poised in the Gulf posed a clear threat to Iraqi forces based in Kuwait and their presence kept Iraqi forces pinned to the coast.

RIGHT: Amphibious operations fall into four broad categories; assaults, raids, demonstrations and withdrawals. The flexibility of maritime power means that the same force may be able to conduct any one of these operations without the need to reconfigure.

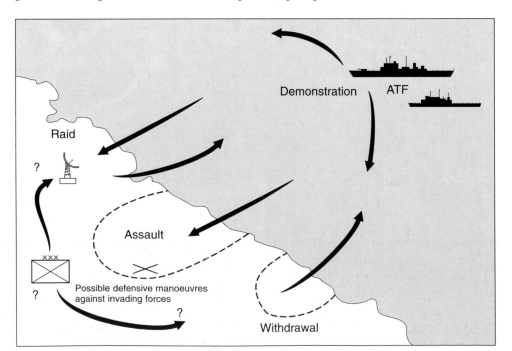

CHAPTER ONE

PLANNING AND PREPARATION

Careful planning and preparation can make the difference between decisive success and bloody failure in amphibious operations.

Amphibious operations are amongst the most complex of all military activities to plan and prepare for, as they require the integration and coordination of a variety of diverse assets. Winston Churchill described amphibious operations as having to 'fit together like a jewelled bracelet'. The first, and most important, stage of any amphibious operation is the planning and preparation. Mistakes at this point will be amplified in later stages and may result in heavy casualties and unfulfilled objectives. Even without enemy interference, amphibious operations are difficult, as forces must often work against natural hazards such as rough seas, difficult surf, strong and variable currents, rocks, sandbars and a bewildering variety of beach conditions before they can get ashore. Once ashore, the build-up of their combat power must be rapid in order to achieve their

LEFT: General Douglas MacArthur (seated) observes the UN landings at Inchon on 15 September 1950 aboard the USS *McKinley*. MacArthur already had extensive experience of amphibious operations, gained in operations against the Japanese in the south-west Pacific and the Philippines during World War II. This, and the experience of his staff, proved vital to the success of the Inchon landings.

ABOVE: US Marines practise an amphibious assault. In the background are LVTP-7A1 amphibious vehicles, while overhead a helicopter flies. Modern amphibious operations require the close integration of air, land and sea assets.

BELOW: Lt Col McCormick lectures on Japanese strength, defences and capabilities during a pre-invasion conference prior to the US assault on Iwo Jima in February 1945.

objectives before powerful enemy forces can intervene. The need to coordinate activities on the land, on the sea and in the air creates many problems. Successful amphibious operations require the close coordination of many different forces, usually from different branches of the armed forces and often between allies. Thus, the amphibious planner has many challenges to overcome.

COMMAND RELATIONSHIPS

The first stage in the planning and preparation of an amphibious assault is the issue of an 'initiating directive'. This is done by a senior commander and it identifies the operation's objectives and assigns the necessary forces, as well as designating the appropriate commanders. The most important of these commanders are the commander of the amphibious task force (CATF) and the commander of the landing force (CLF). The CATF is usually a naval officer and is responsible for the preparation of the amphibious operation's overall plan. The CLF is most often an army officer, or a marine, and is responsible for the planning and conduct of the actual amphibious landing, or assault. It is vital that the CATF and the CLF work closely together and, in order to do this, they are usually co-located when ashore prior to the operation and in the same headquarters vessel when at sea.

One of the enduring problems over the years has been reconciling the requirements of the land battle with those of the war at sea. In the past, command arrangements were often ambiguous, leading to disputes between the navy and the army. Even where there were no disputes, the lack of a single, overall commander often meant that the different services found it hard to coordinate their efforts to maximum effect. For example, unlike the Americans, the British tended to employ 'joint' command, with two officers of equal rank – one from the Army and the other from the Navy – each responsible for their own forces. It was deemed not possible to have a single commander, as it was believed that no one officer could be equally proficient in both land and maritime operations. Unfortunately, this system proved to be unwieldy and

undermined the planning process in a number of operations, notably at Gallipoli in 1915 and at Narvik in Norway in 1940. Consequently, by 1943 the British generally accepted the American approach. This approach recommended the appointment of a single commander in chief who would be responsible for coordinating the requirements of his subordinate commanders representing the land, sea and air elements of his force. This is the approach that is now favoured by most nations.

PREPARATION

One of the first matters to be decided is which forces will be used for the operation. Ideally, the troops employed for the assault phase of the operation should be specially trained and equipped for this role. Examples of these include the United States Marine Corps, the British Royal Marine Commandos and the Royal Netherlands Marine Corps. These forces have a level of experience and expertise unmatched by ordinary troops. In the absence of specialist formations, amphibious operations can be conducted by conventional military units. In such cases, success depends on careful training and also on having access to an appropriate body of expertise which can provide specialist advice and assistance. History has demonstrated time and again the value of experience and specialist training. In large-scale operations where protracted military operations inland are anticipated, even specialist amphibious forces may need to be supplemented by army units. Conventional military forces may be required to provide armour, artillery, logistic support and infantry reinforcements. The requirement to land heavy equipment, such as tanks, artillery and motor transport, may complicate the landing as such equipment is rarely designed to be landed over open beaches. In many cases, port facilities will be needed to land this equipment and capturing these facilities may have to be included in the overall plan.

The next issue to be considered is the training of the forces. The degree of training required depends on the quality of the troops and the difficulty of the planned operation. Specialist amphibious

ABOVE: Dutch Marines conduct an exercise in northern Norway. The Royal Netherlands Marine Corps and the British Royal Marines frequently exercise in the arduous conditions found in Norway, honing their skills and maintaining expertise. These two marine corps have a very close working relationship formalized under the United Kingdom/Netherlands Amphibious Force which was established in 1973.

ABOVE: US Marines conduct a training exercise with a DUKW (amphibious truck) in Virginia during World War II. Training exercises like this were vital if troops were to become familiar with the equipment and tactics required to conduct amphibious operations.

forces which are maintained in a state of readiness may require little or no special training prior to an operation; such forces undergo intense training as a matter of course. The Royal Marine Commandos complete a 30-week-long basic training, the toughest of any infantry force in the world. Likewise, a United States Marine Corps Marine Expeditionary Unit (MEU) must demonstrate its competence in a series of arduous tests before it is considered fit for action and given the Special Operations Capable accreditation. Complex landings involving forces unused to the rigours of an amphibious assault will require a greater degree of preparation. Individual troops need to practise the art of embarkation and disembarkation from landing craft and helicopters, and the naval force must prepare detailed timings for the assault wave as well as for the follow-on forces. All of this may take a considerable period of time. It is often necessary to test the plan and procedures in one or more rehearsals, which are also time-consuming and may, if observed by the enemy, even compromise the security of the whole operation.

The question of which equipment will be used is a complex one. Amphibious operations require a vast amount of

purpose-built equipment, and assaulting forces need craft which can land men, vehicles and equipment within wading depth over a variety of different beach gradients. These craft must be transported to the assault area in larger vessels with greater range and speed which are capable of embarking the assault force. If the landings are expected to be opposed, then the assault wave must be supported by various special craft which will suppress the defenders while the first wave secures the beach. Vehicles belonging to the landing force need waterproofing if they are to be landed across the beach, and the force requires a Beach Armoured Recovery Vehicle (BARV) to recover any vehicles that are flooded and become stranded in the surf.

Special headquarters facilities need to be provided – including provision for controlling air operations and naval fire-support in the battle zone – by a specialist headquarters ship such as the USS *Mount Whitney*; otherwise they may be accommodated in a dual-role amphibious ship or naval vessel.

The force needs to be protected while it is at sea by maritime and air assets. Logistic support, above and beyond that provided by naval vessels, is likely to come from merchant vessels, which are described as Ships Taken Up From Trade (STUFT). In certain circumstances, these merchant vessels may be required to carry the assault troops but, as they lack the capabilities of specialist craft, their use in this role can seriously complicate planning. All of these issues will be examined in greater detail in other chapters later in this book.

CHOOSING A LANDING SITE

Planning for an amphibious operation is complicated by a variety of factors. The most important of these is the nature of the landing force's mission. The nature of the landing force will be determined by the objectives it must achieve inland. As with all military operations, good intelligence is absolutely vital. The fact that the opposing forces are not in physical contact with each other, as is the case in land combat, complicates the collection of intelligence and increases the need for flexibility. The operation is planned backwards, with the requirement for military operations ashore serving to determine the landing site and the forces employed as well as the level of support required. This may be relatively easy, as with a small-scale raid, or incredibly complicated, as with an assault on the scale of the 1944 Normandy landings.

In traditional amphibious assaults, the initial objective of the landing force is to secure the landing site, usually a beach. Having done this, the landing site will be consolidated and a beachhead will be built up to ensure the space and facilities for the landing of more troops and equipment. Choice of the landing site will depend on both the type of operation being conducted and the tactical requirement to land sufficient troops and equipment to achieve their objectives inland. There is no such thing as an ideal landing site, as the most suitable beaches are often either too far away from the ultimate objectives or too heavily defended.

Many factors influence the choice of landing site. The beach must have the capacity for landing supplies and equipment once it has been secured by the initial assault. The offshore approaches must be navigable, and the presence of mines and underwater obstacles may influence this. The landing site will have to be suitable for beaching landing ships and craft as well as for operating amphibious assault vehicles. Beaches with a steep gradient offer a better chance of a dry landing as well as reducing the risk of landing craft being stranded by an ebb tide. Wide beaches allow for a large assault-wave to land in line abreast. There must be sufficient space to build up stores and equipment within the beachhead. In addition, there must be suitable exits to

BELOW: German troops practise unloading a cart from an improvised landing craft in 1940. With the exception of the Panzer units much of the German Army's transport remained horse-drawn throughout the war. Landing craft such as these were made from hastily converted barges and river boats.

ABOVE: US transports and landing craft were markedly more sophisticated than their German counterparts during World War II.

BELOW: The Amphibious Command Ship USS *Mount Whitney* off the coast of Haiti during Operation Support Democracy in July 1994.

allow troops and equipment to move inland. Land communications need to be established to allow the landing force to progress further inland in order to achieve their objectives. As such, the nature of the terrain inland from the beach will be an important consideration.

The strength, capabilities and disposition of enemy forces are of fundamental importance. Ideally, an unopposed landing is preferable, although it is not always possible. Opposed landings are

traditionally difficult and costly but they can often achieve dramatic results. Only forces that are extremely well trained, well equipped and well led can hope to succeed against a well-entrenched opponent. It is very doubtful whether any force – except perhaps that of the United States Marine Corps – has the ability to do this at the present time.

From the 1950s, the use of the helicopter has broadened the range of landing sites available to the amphibious

commander. Factors to consider when choosing a helicopter landing site include the number of helicopters available for landing operations, as well as their range, speed and payload. The more helicopters that are available the larger the initial troop lift can be. The availability of helicopter routes to and from the landing site is also an important consideration.

These routes may be limited by geographic factors such as high mountains, or by enemy activity such as anti-aircraft fire. The number and location of enemy anti-aircraft positions may influence the choice of route. The distance from the helicopter's mother ship to the landing site is important. Extended range requires a greater fuel

BELOW: When planning an amphibious operation numerous factors must be considered, which may conflict with each other; there is no such thing as a perfect landing site. A commander must choose the best compromise between conflicting priorities.

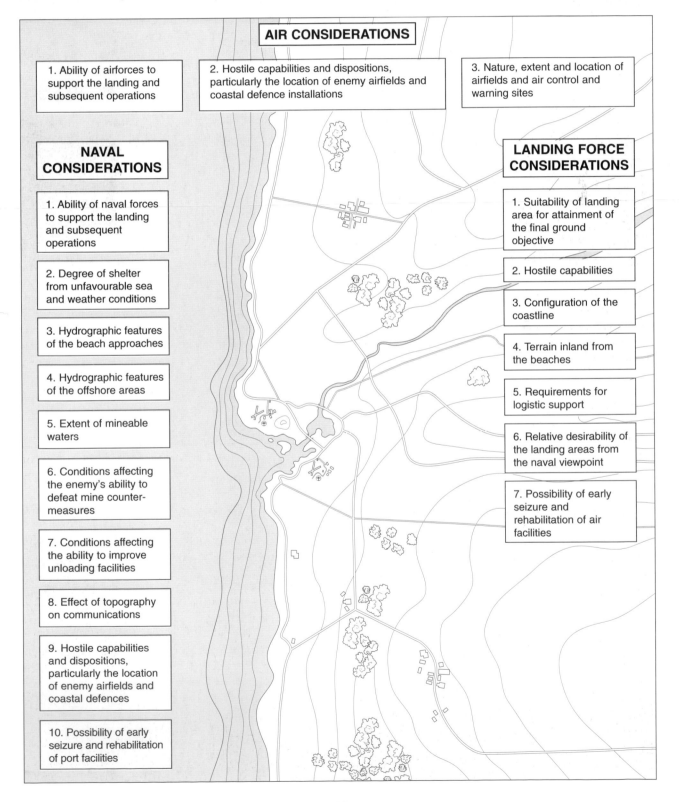

AIR CONSIDERATIONS

1. Ability of airforces to support the landing and subsequent operations

2. Hostile capabilities and dispositions, particularly the location of enemy airfields and coastal defence installations

3. Nature, extent and location of airfields and air control and warning sites

NAVAL CONSIDERATIONS

1. Ability of naval forces to support the landing and subsequent operations

2. Degree of shelter from unfavourable sea and weather conditions

3. Hydrographic features of the beach approaches

4. Hydrographic features of the offshore areas

5. Extent of mineable waters

6. Conditions affecting the enemy's ability to defeat mine counter-measures

7. Conditions affecting the ability to improve unloading facilities

8. Effect of topography on communications

9. Hostile capabilities and dispositions, particularly the location of enemy airfields and coastal defences

10. Possibility of early seizure and rehabilitation of port facilities

LANDING FORCE CONSIDERATIONS

1. Suitability of landing area for attainment of the final ground objective

2. Hostile capabilities

3. Configuration of the coastline

4. Terrain inland from the beaches

5. Requirements for logistic support

6. Relative desirability of the landing areas from the naval viewpoint

7. Possibility of early seizure and rehabilitation of air facilities

ABOVE: US LSTs unload supplies onto the beach at Inchon in September 1950. The ability to land supplies and reinforcements and to evacuate wounded personnel is of critical importance.

load and this reduces the overall payload of the helicopter. The ability to sustain and support a helicopter-landed force once ashore is a vital consideration. Helicopters are very versatile, but, even so, they are not able to carry as many supplies as conventional landing craft, and this is a factor which is exacerbated by extended range. Finally, the landing force must be able to identify the chosen landing site from the air. Misidentification is easy under combat conditions and it can lead to disaster.

'TIME AND TIDE...'

The timing of an amphibious landing is of critical importance and will differ from case to case. The concept of operations ashore will be the determining factor, along with the requirement to coordinate supporting arms. Operations that rely on stealth and surprise, such as raids, are best conducted at night. Larger, more complex operations, requiring the integration of a variety of different forces, may need to be conducted in daylight. However, feints and diversions are, by their nature, supposed to be detected by the enemy and are therefore most often conducted during the day.

Other factors to be considered include the local conditions of tide and current. A landing undertaken at high tide will reduce the length of open beach that the assault-wave must cross. Alternatively, a landing which takes place at low tide provides a greater depth of beach in which to organize the landed force and it also allows beached landing craft to re-float on the rising tide. Weather conditions are always important, as beach landings and helicopter operations are difficult in bad weather, and the state of the moon will determine the degree of darkness at night which may also influence timings. Another important consideration is the enemy routines, and this is true particularly if defending forces are known to be on alert at particular times. However, the need for tactical surprise may compromise these principles. For example, the landing force may wish to land at dusk in order to develop the beachhead under cover of darkness, but a surprise attack may dictate that the landing ships move towards the beach at night, and because of this the actual assault may have to take place at daybreak.

CASE STUDY: OPERATION OVERLORD, 6 JUNE 1944

The Allied landing in Normandy, codenamed Operation Overlord, was the largest and most complex amphibious operation of all time. On 6 June 1944, five allied divisions stormed ashore to breach a hole in Hitler's vaunted Fortress Europe. The amphibious assault was supported by three airborne divisions, dropped under cover of darkness the night before the main landing. In total, 133,000 men were landed from the sea with a further 23,000 arriving by parachute or glider. By midnight on D-Day, the Eastern (British) Task Force

alone had landed 900 tanks and armoured vehicles and 520 anti-tank guns and artillery pieces. The landings required over 2000 landing ships and craft and they were supported by 11,590 Allied aircraft and a naval force that included seven battleships, 23 cruisers and more than 100 destroyers.

The planning process for an operation on this scale was inevitably lengthy and complex. Initial preparations had begun as early as 1940 when the British had established the Combined Operations Headquarters in order to examine the requirements for future operations. Detailed planning began in 1943 when Lieutenant-General Morgan was appointed Chief of Staff to the Supreme Allied Commander (designate). As the United States would eventually provide the majority of the forces in north-west Europe, an American general, General Dwight D. Eisenhower, was appointed as Supreme Commander. Below him were the three British commanders of the land, sea and air forces for Overlord, General Bernard Montgomery, Admiral Bertram Ramsay and Air Marshal Trafford Leigh-Mallory. Admiral Ramsay

BELOW: Decisions about the date and time for an amphibious landing are as complex as the choice of the actual site. Certain planning criteria can be identified but it may be difficult to fulfil all criteria in all operations. Inevitably priorities have to be established and different criteria may be considered at the expense of others.

DATE FOR LANDING

S	M	T	W	T	F	S
o	1	2	3	4	5	6
7	8	9	10	11	12	13
14	15	16	17	18	19	20
21	22	23	24	25	26	27
28	29	30				

HOUR FOR LANDING

- Availability of forces
- Readiness of forces
- Present and projected enemy situation
- Seasonal conditions in the area under consideration
- Local conditions of weather, tide, current, phase of moon (duration of darkness and daylight)
- Designation of limiting dates by a higher authority
- Coordination with preliminary operations

- Known enemy routine
- Duration of daylight
- Need for tactical surprise
- Concept of operations ashore of the landing force
- Favourable conditions of wind, tide and the phase of the moon
- Requirements for conducting certain operations during hours of darkness
- Most effective employment of air and naval gunfire support

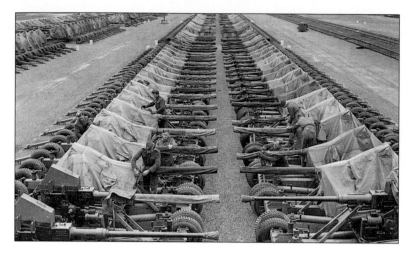

ABOVE: At an equipment depot 'somewhere in England' 1.5in (40mm) Bofors light anti-aircraft guns are stored prior to their use in the forthcoming invasion of France. The Allied invasion of France in 1944 relied on massive stocks of shells, guns and equipment and these were stored in ordnance, ammunition and vehicle depots across Britain.

joined the planning staff for Overlord in October 1943 and he was joined by the remaining commanders later in the year. It is a measure of the complexity of the planning process that the naval orders prepared by Ramsay and issued prior to the operations ran to a total of 1000 pages of foolscap print. Similar orders issued prior to the British landing at Gallipoli in 1915 had amounted to only about 30 pages.

The key question facing the planning team was the choice of landing area, and

this issue generated considerable debate. The collection of data on potential landing beaches began in 1941, and at this point intelligence was gathered from a variety of sources, including pre-war tide tables, Michelin tourist guides, postcards and holiday snaps, in addition to more conventional military means such as photographic reconnaissance, special-forces operations and local intelligence from the French Resistance. Tides, currents, beach gradients and the topography inland were all considered. The Pas de Calais region benefited from its proximity to the south coast of Britain and was an obvious base for an advance into the heartland of Germany, and consequently the Germans had concentrated their defences there. In addition, there were few beaches suitable for a major assault, therefore the planners chose an alternative site further to the west at Normandy. This area offered the advantage of having suitable landing beaches and of being away from the main concentration of German forces, but it was still within the range of the Spitfire fighters which were based in southern Britain. The decision to land at

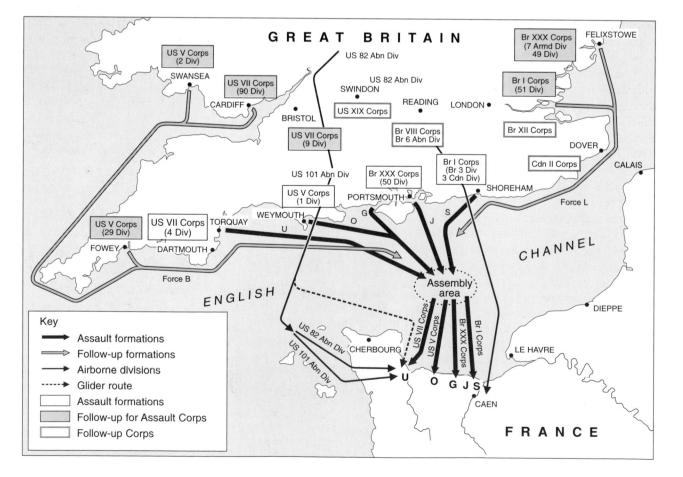

Normandy was approved at the Quebec Conference in August 1943.

The original plan developed in 1943 catered for an assault by three divisions landing between Caen and Carentan. Montgomery and Eisenhower both considered this to be inadequate and consequently the plan was eventually stretched to include five divisions landed by sea, with a further three airborne divisions landed to secure the flanks of the invasion force. One division, the US 4th Infantry, was to land on the east coast of the Cotentin peninsula for the capture of Cherbourg. The desire to seize Cherbourg at the first opportunity demonstrated exactly how preoccupied the planners were with capturing a major port so that the supply and reinforcement of the landing force could be guaranteed. It was these concerns, as well as the realization that a port could not be taken in the initial assault, that led to the development of the artificial harbours that were towed across the channel and subsequently established at Arromanche and St Laurent.

The timing of the landing caused much debate. The Army wanted to land at night in order to maximize the element of surprise. However, the Navy wanted to land in daylight in order to ensure the proper control and coordination of all the maritime assets. In the event, there was a compromise; the Army accepted a landing at first light, six and a half hours after the first airborne landings at midnight (British Summer Time). Weather conditions were an important consideration. The original date for D-Day had been 5 June 1944. However, on 1 June the tranquil summer weather in the English Channel was replaced by a vicious storm. Because of this, on 4 June Eisenhower was forced to delay the landings by 24 hours. However, Allied meteorologists predicted that the storms would clear on 6 June and thus Eisenhower was able to order the landings to proceed as before, although they were one day late. The storm had an unexpected bonus: Allied control of the sea and air meant that the Germans did not have access to the same data as the Allies and so they were unaware that the weather would clear. Consequently, believing that an amphibious assault would not be possible for some days,

many senior commanders were away from their commands on the morning of the invasion, including Field Marshal Rommel, Commander of Army Group B and one of Hitler's most gifted generals.

The planners who prepared for and conducted the Normandy landings did their job exceptionally well. Their work has justly been described as a 'never surpassed masterpiece of planning'. All of the potential variables – weather, topography, geography, beach conditions, tidal states, enemy dispositions and reactions and Allied capabilities – were assessed and catered for. This was possible due to the extended build-up prior to the invasion and the unprecedented scale of resources made available. The success at Normandy was to seal the fate of Nazi Germany and was also to lead to the liberation of Western Europe. Failure would have been a disaster; the efforts of Eisenhower and his subordinates, however, ensured that the chances of this happening were minimized.

CASE STUDY: GERMANY AND AMPHIBIOUS WARFARE, 1940

The Normandy landings succeeded because of the Allies' careful planning and preparation, and because of the allocation of overwhelming resources. Studying German plans for the invasion of Britain in 1940 demonstrates some of the difficulties in conducting amphibious operations when most of the traditional planning criteria are absent. Prior to 1940, Germany had no history or experience of amphibious operations. In April 1940 Germany successfully invaded neutral Norway, despite the lack of a

FAR LEFT, BOTTOM: This map illustrates the disposition of British, American and Canadian forces in England prior to the invasion and their routes to the assault area. By May 1944 the south of England was host to an enormous collection of troops, vehicles and equipment, and the ports and harbours of the south coast were congested with landing ships and craft.

BELOW: US troops march through the streets of a British town on their way to an embarkation port on the south coast of England. The build-up of US forces in Britain was a vital pre-requisite for the Normandy landings. By May 1944 over one and a half million American troops had crossed the Atlantic and were preparing for operations against Germany.

ABOVE: An English port in Spring 1944, prior to the invasion of Normandy. Over 2000 amphibious ships and craft were required for the Normandy landings. These had to be loaded in tactical order and then sailed in convoy to the invasion area, before landing their embarked load on the right beach at the right time.

specialist amphibious capability. That operation relied upon surprise, massive air superiority and a high degree of luck. However, success came at a price; the German Navy lost three cruisers and 10 destroyers sunk, and three battleships and two cruisers damaged. This further undermined its already inferior position vis-à-vis the British Royal Navy and was to seriously complicate future plans to invade Britain.

Prior to the fall of France in June 1940, both the German Army and Navy had considered the possibility of invading Britain. Admiral Raeder identified the east coast of England as the most favourable landing area but concluded that, due to the weakness of Germany's naval forces and its lack of a specialist amphibious capability, an invasion could not be recommended. Initial army studies anticipated landing 17 divisions on the east coast, in East Anglia, with diversionary landings further north. After more study, in May 1940 the naval planning team concluded that a cross-Channel landing was preferable to a landing on the east coast. The southern coast of England offered less favourable landing beaches and was not as well placed for subsequent operations against London, but in the narrow seas of the English Channel the invasion force might more easily be defended by a combination of mine barriers and both naval and air forces.

A key constraint on German planning was the lack of any specialist amphibious shipping, so hundreds of river barges and other small craft were collected from the coastlines and inland waterways of occupied Europe. Many of these were converted into makeshift landing craft by the addition of bow ramps which were suitable for landing vehicles. With no experience of amphibious operations, the Army consistently underestimated the difficulty of transporting and landing this force. Some officers expressed the view that the operation was actually no more difficult than an opposed river crossing.

On 16 July 1940 Hitler issued Führer Directive No. 16, formally ordering preparations for the invasion to begin. The operation was codenamed Seelöwe (Sealion). Hitler did not designate an overall commander; neither did he create a central planning staff. As a consequence, disputes between the Army and the Navy planning teams continued. The original plan called for the landing of 13 divisions on the southern coast of England on a broad front of 237 miles (391km). This would take place over a three-day period and it was to eventually be built up to a strength of 40 divisions. However, this was not realistic. Admiral Raeder estimated that it would take at least 10 days to land such a force and that a landing on a broad front would, in any case, be impossible to protect. The Navy favoured a smaller landing on a narrow front. As a consequence, in the German plans, the landing force contracted to 10 divisions on a 100-mile (160km) front, and then to six divisions over three days on an 80-mile (128km) front between Bexhill and Worthing. The landings would be supported by one airborne division and an air-landed division who were to capture the port of Folkestone.

Planning proceeded in an air of unreality. The slow speed of the makeshift amphibious force meant that it would take at least 15 hours to cross the Channel. Once offshore, it would take 36 hours to ferry the assaulting divisions ashore. Even if the Luftwaffe were able to secure complete air superiority, Royal Navy destroyers were liable to penetrate the minefields which protected either flank of the invasion fleet and then wreak havoc amongst the vulnerable shipping stationed offshore. Casualties were likely to be high. With a limited amount of combat strength ashore in the early stages of the assault, German forces in England would be extremely vulnerable to any counter-attack. The German Army Chief of Staff, General Halder, was not alone in his objections when he described the plan for Sealöwe as being suicidal.

In the event, the Germans did not carry out Operation Sealöwe. The entire plan depended upon the Luftwaffe gaining air superiority over the Channel and southern England, and their attempt to achieve this was defeated by the Royal Air Force in the Battle of Britain. On 12 October Operation Sealöwe was postponed indefinitely. There is some doubt as to whether Hitler was ever serious about the operation, as he did not invest any personal credibility in the invasion plans. Preparation for Operation Sealöwe may have been part of an elaborate bluff intended to coerce Britain into accepting a negotiated peace. It is doubtful whether we will ever know the truth over this issue, but what is clear is the fact that in 1940 the German armed forces certainly did not have the training, the experience or the resources to plan and conduct an amphibious operation on this scale with any reasonable prospect of achieving success.

CASE STUDY: OPERATION CHROMITE – THE INCHON LANDING, 1950

Major amphibious landings usually require an extended period of planning and preparation but circumstances do not always allow for this. The assault landing at Inchon on the west coast of Korea was one of the most difficult and dangerous operations of that war. The landing was

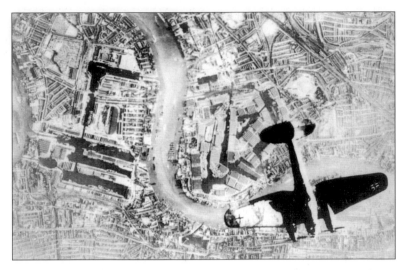

entirely successful, severing North Korean communications to their forces in the south and facilitating the breakout of United Nations forces from their tenuous bridgehead around Pusan. The landing was also planned and conducted at extremely short notice and it is an example of the great value of both experience and expertise.

The key figure in this episode was General Douglas MacArthur. MacArthur had commanded US forces in the south-west Pacific during World War II and had conducted a series of successful amphibious operations. As soon as he was appointed to command UN forces in Korea on 10 July 1950, he began to investigate the potential use of amphibious operations to stem the North Korean advance. The geography of Korea – a long peninsula with land communications concentrated along the coastline – made it particularly vulnerable to attacks from maritime power. By August 1950 the North Korean advance had been stopped just short of the southern port of Pusan. Conventional wisdom suggested the protracted build-up of UN strength within the limited bridgehead at Pusan, followed by a land advance north in order to recapture lost territory. However, General MacArthur thought otherwise. He wanted to use amphibious forces to seize territory behind the Communist armies in the south, cutting their lines of communications and facilitating the breakout of forces from Pusan.

A variety of landing sites were investigated. Potential sites on the east coast included Chinnampo in the north

ABOVE: A German He-111 bomber flies over the docklands in the East End of London in 1940. The inability of the German Luftwaffe to achieve air superiority over the RAF in the Battle of Britain destroyed any chance of a German invasion of Britain.

ABOVE: Barges gather in German-occupied Channel ports ready for use in Operation Sealion. The lack of a proper amphibious capability forced the Germans to requisition a number of river barges and coastal craft and to press them into service as makeshift landing craft. The slow speed, limited payload and poor sea-keeping of most of these vessels made this a very unsatisfactory amphibious fleet.

and Kunsan in the south. Both were rejected, Chinnampo as it was too deep in enemy territory, and Kunsan because it was too close to the Pusan perimeter. A landing at Kunsan would have had some advantages; it would have allowed for mutual support between the landing force and the 8th Army at Pusan. However, it would also give the Koreans the advantage of interior lines, allowing them to switch resources between Kunsan and Pusan and to contain the beachhead in the same way that the Germans had contained the Allied landing at Anzio in 1944. The landing site favoured by MacArthur was Inchon, the port that served the occupied South Korean capital, Seoul. Inchon offered the potential of a deep envelopment, cutting enemy communications and lines of supply to the south and posing a real threat to North Korean rear areas. In addition, it had the political advantage of the early liberation of Seoul.

In terms of conventional planning criteria, Inchon was not an ideal choice. The tidal range was around 30ft (9.1m), leaving 6000yds (5486m) of impassable mud flats exposed at low tide. US landing

ships required 29ft (8.8m) of water under their keel but tides of this height were only available for four days a month. The need to land at high tide meant that tidal conditions would determine not only the day of the landing but also the time of the landing. In addition, currents in the approach channels were very strong, varying between 3 and 7 knots, not much less than the top speed of a landing craft. The main approach to the harbour, known as 'Flying Fish Channel', was narrow and difficult to navigate and this effectively ruled out an approach in darkness. It would only take one ship to be sunk in this channel for it to be blocked to further traffic, and it was also very vulnerable to mining. The whole harbour area was dominated by a fortified island, Wolmi-do, and this would have to be neutralized before any landing could take place. As if this was not enough, there were no actual beaches at Inchon; the assault wave would have to land directly into the heart of the city over narrow and congested sea walls ranging in height from 12 to 14ft (3.6–4.2m). Planning was further complicated by the lack of any detailed and accurate intelligence about conditions at Inchon.

The urgency to reverse the tide of the war in the UN's favour left little time for extended preparations. MacArthur announced the plan to land at Inchon, which was codenamed Operation Chromite, on 12 August. Tidal conditions at Inchon dictated a landing on either 15 September or 11 October, and the earlier date was chosen. However, US doctrine suggested that the planning period should be 90 days long!

The planning team consisted of Vice Admiral Struble, Rear Admiral Doyle and Major General Oliver P. Smith. Smith, who was to command 1st US Marine Division – the formation conducting the assault – did not join the planning team in Japan until 22 August, giving him little more than 20 days both to prepare for and plan the complex, opposed landing. Fortunately, the planning team shared a wealth of experience in amphibious operations. Both Doyle and Smith had gained extensive experience against the Japanese during the successful campaign across the Central Pacific in World War II, while Struble had experience of operations at Normandy and in the south-west Pacific. Without this expertise, it is doubtful whether Operation Chromite could have been devised at such short notice.

Their plan was unusual: there would be an initial assault to take the island of Wolmi-do on the morning tide, enabling the remainder of the landing force to assault Inchon itself on the evening tide 12 hours later. To stop the North Koreans from reinforcing Inchon during the intervening period, and to suppress any defenders in the town, maximum support would be provided by the guns and aircraft of the fleet. A diversionary landing at Kunsan was designed to confuse the enemy as to the exact location of the main operation.

The 1st US Marine Division included many veterans of World War II. Despite the unusual challenges they faced, the marines carried out their orders and achieved all of their objectives. Inchon was taken and UN forces reoccupied Seoul on 26 September. With their lines of communication cut, the Communist forces in the South collapsed once the advance from Pusan began. Only the eventual intervention of China on the side of North Korea prevented a UN victory and the reunification of Korea.

CONCLUSION

Amphibious operations are amongst the most difficult operations to plan and prepare for because of the unique challenges faced when projecting power from the sea. Ideally, commanders will have sufficient time and resources to plan and prepare an operation in order to minimize the inevitable problems, but this is not always possible. Operation Chromite demonstrated that, while there may be certain planning guidelines that the amphibious commander ignores at their peril, there are no fixed rules. An experienced commander who is supported by an efficient staff and in command of well-trained and properly equipped forces may be able to overcome seemingly insurmountable obstacles. However, this will only be possible if the appropriate knowledge, skills and equipment are also present. The factors outlined at the start of this chapter will always be important and the ability of the commander to overcome the challenges that these pose will determine the overall success of the operation.

BELOW: US Marines prepare ammunition for their tank, embarked in a US landing ship off Korea in 1950. By 1950 the US had decommissioned much of its huge World War II fleet of amphibious ships. Fortunately, enough specialist shipping remained in service or in reserve to support the Inchon landings and subsequent operations.

CHAPTER TWO

PASSAGE TO THE BATTLE ZONE

Crowded into transports, it is during transit that the amphibious task force may be at its most vulnerable.

The passage to the battle zone is defined as the period during which, after planning has been executed and the force assembled, the components of the amphibious task force move either from their points of embarkation or from forward deployed positions to the Amphibious Objective Area (AOA), the area of operations. A successful passage to the battle zone is a pre-requisite of a successful operation; in other words, if the Amphibious Task Force (ATF) cannot get to the area of operation, then the operation cannot take place. Even if the ATF gets to the battle zone, damage en route can jeopardize the outcome of the subsequent amphibious landing. The length of the journey from the areas of embarkation to the area of operations can vary. Limited operations, along the lines of a Soviet desant of World War II and similar tactical coastal landings, may

LEFT: US LVTs pass a line of LCI(G) bombardment craft on their way towards the shore during the landings on Peleliu, 15 September 1944. The US Navy's victory over the Japanese at the Battle of the Philippine Sea in June 1944 had seen the Japanese aircraft carrier fleet finally removed as a serious threat to Allied amphibious operations.

BELOW: British soldiers embark for the 8000-mile (12,870km) passage from the United Kingdom to the Falkland Islands in 1982. Few navies have the capability to conduct operations at such extended range. In 1982 the British were considerably aided by the inability of the Argentine Navy or Airforce to attack the vulnerable shipping during its long passage south.

involve relatively short transit distances, but often the distances to be travelled are much greater. In Operation Overlord, for example, forces had to transit 80 miles (128km), and for the assault on Narvik in 1940 German forces were shipped over 800 miles (1280km). During the Pacific 'island hopping' campaign of World War II, the Falklands war of 1982 and the Gulf War of 1990–1, the distances were often measured in thousands of miles. The passage phase of an amphibious operation is a point of acute potential vulnerability, where transport ships which are crammed with troops, equipment, and supplies face the depredations of the weather, chance and enemy action. The transit period may also be critical for creating and/or sustaining the important element of surprise in an operation with, for example, the use of diversionary operations and feints.

CHALLENGES

Amphibious forces may face threats even before they have embarked. The opposition may try to attack embarkation points as a way of disrupting preparations, as was the case with British bombing raids against Channel ports during the threatened German invasion of 1940. Then, as it transits from its embarkation points towards the battle zone, the amphibious force is threatened by a wide range of dangers: weather, dangerous geographic 'choke-points', logistic difficulties, and command and control over what might be widely dispersed forces. Time may also be an important challenge, as it was for the British during the Suez operation in 1956, where growing international political opposition to the operation was the main threat. The severity of these problems will vary greatly depending upon the context of the operation: the size of the amphibious

force; the political environment; the geography of the transit route; the time of year and so on.

THREATS IN TRANSIT

However, chief amongst the potential dangers facing the amphibious task force are the maritime forces of the opposition. If technological developments during the 20th century have given the amphibious force a range of potential defensive capabilities, from submarine screens to carrier-based aircraft, the scope of possible threats which face transiting forces has also widened, from sophisticated mines to long-range surface attack missiles and high-capability surveillance systems. A key factor in the success of the passage to the battle zone is sufficient sea control, which is defined as a situation in which a maritime force can use the sea for its own purposes and deny its use to the enemy, in a specified area and for a specified period of time. Where sea control is unlimited in time and space, it is often referred to as 'command of the sea'. 'Sea denial' is a term widely used to describe the process of challenging an enemy's sea control. If the amphibious task force is moving through an area without sufficient sea control, then damaging attrition is always a possibility. The degree of challenge to control the battle space around the amphibious force will vary, and it depends upon the nature of the conflict, as well as the strength and capabilities of the opposition. At the extreme, for example, in projected Cold War operations against the Soviet Union,

likely threats to NATO amphibious force in transit would have been extensive: submarine attack through torpedoes and cruise missiles; long-range Backfire bombers; Soviet surface action groups; and then, as the amphibious task group moved into the coastal area offshore/inshore defence forces, mines and small missile-firing fast attack boats. In other circumstances, surprise, prior action against the enemy's maritime forces, or a lack of enemy capabilities in the first place may render the challenge to sea control minimal. US forces moving against Grenada in 1983 faced no significant threat as they went forward to the area of amphibious operations because of Grenada's lack of substantial sea-denial capability.

Whatever the dangers, in order for the amphibious operation to succeed, the transiting force must avoid a critical reduction in its combat potential, since this might threaten – or even destroy completely – the chances of success for the following amphibious operations. Several factors need to be taken into consideration to ensure that the forces in transit suffer the minimum amount of attrition possible.

THE CHOICE OF ROUTE

One factor is the choice of route. The amphibious task force should be able to move forward without unnecessary interference and so, where practicable, historically commanders have avoided areas of water that could be mined or that posed navigational hazards. They have

ABOVE: The US carriers USS *Ticonderoga* and USS *Langley* enter Ulithi anchorage in December 1944 after launching airstrikes against Japanese facilities in the Philippines. The great carrier battles of the Coral Sea (1942), Midway (1942) and the Philippine Sea (1944) saw the destruction of the once dominant Japanese carrier force and allowed US carriers to conduct offensive operations against the land.

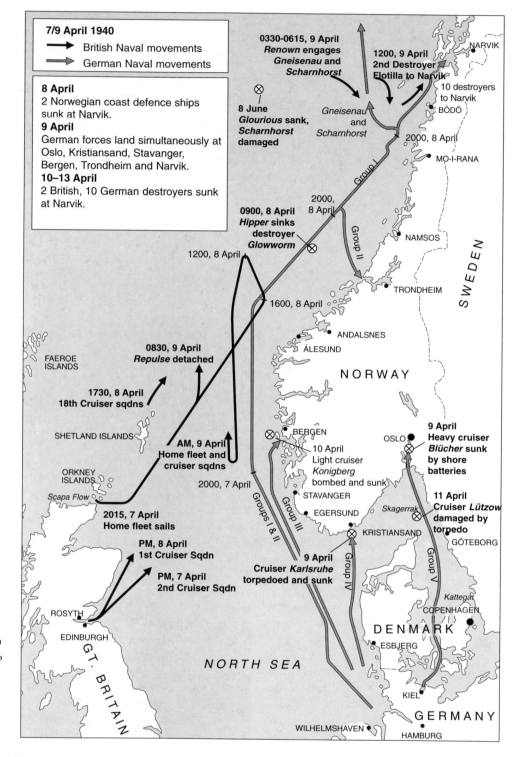

7/9 April 1940
→ British Naval movements
→ German Naval movements

8 April
2 Norwegian coast defence ships sunk at Narvik.
9 April
German forces land simultaneously at Oslo, Kristiansand, Stavanger, Bergen, Trondheim and Narvik.
10–13 April
2 British, 10 German destroyers sunk at Narvik.

0330-0615, 9 April
Renown engages *Gneisenau* and *Scharnhorst*

NARVIK

1200, 9 April
2nd Destroyer Flotilla to Narvik

10 destroyers to Narvik

BÖDÖ

8 June
Glourious sank, *Scharnhorst* damaged

Gneisenau and *Scharnhorst*

2000, 8 April

MO-I-RANA

Group I

0900, 8 April
Hipper sinks destroyer *Glowworm*

2000, 8 April

Group II

NAMSOS

1200, 8 April

TRONDHEIM

1600, 8 April

SWEDEN

ANDALSNES
ÅLESUND

0830, 9 April
Repulse detached

NORWAY

FAEROE ISLANDS

1730, 8 April
18th Cruiser sqdns

SHETLAND ISLANDS

BERGEN

10 April
Light cruiser *Konigberg* bombed and sunk

OSLO

9 April
Heavy cruiser *Blücher* sunk by shore batteries

AM, 9 April
Home fleet and cruiser sqdns

2000, 7 April

Groups I & II

Group III

STAVANGER

EGERSUND

Skagerrak

11 April
Cruiser *Lützow* damaged by torpedo

GÖTEBORG

ORKNEY ISLANDS

Scapa Flow

2015, 7 April
Home fleet sails

Group IV

KRISTIANSAND

Group V

PM, 8 April
1st Cruiser Sqdn

9 April
Cruiser *Karlsruhe* torpedoed and sunk

PM, 7 April
2nd Cruiser Sqdn

Kattegat

COPENHAGEN

ROSYTH

EDINBURGH

GT. BRITAIN

DENMARK

ESBJERG

NORTH SEA

KIEL

GERMANY

WILHELMSHAVEN

HAMBURG

RIGHT: This map shows the routes taken by the German task groups to Norway. The Germans placed their faith in deception and simultaneity to avoid enemy interception. Even so, the groups destined for Trondheim and Narvik had to run the gauntlet of British attack.

also avoided geographic choke-points or routes that brought the amphibious force within range of enemy land-based missiles or air defences or coastal forces. There needs to be sufficient space in the transit area to allow dispersion of forces, to prevent bunching and to allow the amphibious force to be covered effectively by screening forces. For these reasons, regions such as the Mediterranean, the Baltic and the Persian Gulf have historically proved to be problematic transit areas. The route chosen for the amphibious force also needs to be coordinated with the routes assigned to supporting Maritime Task Groups in order to ensure that the amphibious force is afforded adequate protection at all times.

Another factor to consider in safeguarding the forces in transit is logistics. An amphibious task force makes

LEFT: German soldiers disembark on the shores of Norway in April 1940. The Germans took a calculated risk in their planning that almost did not pay off.

enormous calls on logistics, especially fuel and drinking water. This problem is compounded by the often limited opportunity to resupply the force en route. It is therefore useful to move the amphibious force via staging areas such as bases or pre-designated rendezvous points in order to facilitate logistic resupply and force reorganization. Establishing forward pre-positioned equipment and supply sources can help alleviate some of these problems and may also speed the deployment of the amphibious task force, some elements of which may then be moved by air.

COMPOSITION OF THE TASK FORCE

Another consideration is the composition of the various task groups of the amphibious force, and the order in which they sail to reach the battle zone. This is partly determined by the characteristics of the vessels, such as their speed and armament. Their movement is organized to help the landing operations by ensuring that the right forces arrive at the right time. In the invasion of Norway in 1940, the German heavy equipment was sent ahead of the troops because it was being carried in slow-moving merchant ships, with the troops themselves sailing later on faster-moving warships. The Germans relied on deception and surprise to avoid the elimination of these vulnerable merchant ships. The forces designed to launch and protect the amphibious assault therefore usually consist of one or more of the following:

an Amphibious Group, comprising amphibious shipping, fire-support and escort units; a Transport Group, with STUFT and auxiliary ships; an Escort Group; and a Command/Carrier Task Group with carriers, escort and replenishment ships. For the invasion of Norway, the Germans organized a Transport Group which comprised seven merchant ships and three Naval Transport Squadrons with a total of 38 merchant ships which carried the heavy equipment. The troops themselves went

BELOW: A US aircraft carrier in transit during Operation Desert Storm. Even if Coalition land-based air power had not been so dominant, the US carrier fleet was sufficiently powerful to provide air cover for forces moving into the Gulf.

RIGHT: A US Navy Dauntless on completion of a patrol off the island of Guadalcanal. The USS *Enterprise* is in the foreground, and the USS *Saratoga* is in the distance. At Guadalcanal, the threat from Japanese land-based aircraft forced the US carriers to a position some way from the island. Both Japanese and US reinforcements to Guadalcanal were subject to numerous attacks.

on warships, formed into six task groups, the largest consisting of the two battleships and 10 destroyers with 2000 troops, and the smallest with four minesweepers with 150 troops. The amphibious force may also deploy an Advance Group, which is tasked with reaching the battle zone before the landing and carrying out preliminary work such as degrading enemy defences, blockading, capturing peripheral islands, or screening the advance of the main amphibious force.

If time or conditions allow, there may be scope for carrying out useful tasks en route. These may include training or rehearsals by elements of the amphibious force testing evolutions, such as unloading supplies and ship-to-shore movement. Elements of the escorting support and carrier forces may use the time to exercise against one another in order to identify and remedy weaknesses. If possible, there is at least one rehearsal of the assault phase of the operation. Planning and staff rehearsals can also be used at this stage to hone command and control systems and to refine the plan of assault. The passage to the battle zone is also an opportunity to give pre-operational briefings in order to ensure that every element of the amphibious task force is absolutely clear about its particular function.

THE ESCORT SCREEN

Another factor to consider is that of protection. Amphibious forces can be exceedingly vulnerable given that they may be slow-moving and may include a substantial number of STUFT or other ships with low defensive capabilities. A number of measures may be used to ensure the protection of the amphibious force. Surprise is one option; moving the amphibious forces at an unexpected time or through an unexpected route may manage to avoid the enemy completely. Diversionary forces may be used to draw the enemy away from the intended area of operations. As a rule, however, amphibious forces rely fundamentally on their Maritime Task Group – the submarines, Carrier Task Group, close escorts and so on – to find and deal with enemy forces and protect the assets which are critical to the amphibious mission.

An effective defence of the amphibious force usually has two attributes. First, it is 'layered'; in other words, it includes attack and defence capabilities with a variety of ranges, from close-in defence to long-range reconnaissance and attack. The outer layer may consist of a submarine screen and cover provided by land-based aircraft. Forces which are not part of the amphibious task force may also be used: separate surface groups may undertake supporting operations such as minesweeping, the interdiction of enemy surface ships, or anti-submarine operations; land- or carrier-based aircraft can be used to ensure air superiority over the areas which are to be moved through, or to conduct anti-submarine or anti-surface warfare. Some or all of the support and carrier groups may be attached directly to the transport and landing groups to protect them during the passage. Forward elements of the naval force may include a carrier group with a close escort of air-defence frigates and more widely spread anti-submarine frigate and destroyer escorts.

BATTLESPACE DOMINANCE

The second attribute of an effective defence of the amphibious force is that it needs to extend into all environments. This is referred to in modern terminology as 'battlespace dominance'; that is, control of the surface, subsurface, air, space and electro-magnetic environments around the amphibious task force. For this reason, protecting an amphibious force is best entrusted to a balanced force which is able to meet the enemy in each of these environments. A Carrier Task Group and/or land-based air can provide combat air patrols over the amphibious force, Airborne Early Warning (AEW) and anti-submarine helicopters, as well as anti-surface warfare capabilities. An Escort force ideally includes a mix of ships which are able to protect the amphibious shipping against enemy air and missile attack, submarines, surface vessels, electronic warfare and surveillance.

CASE STUDY: THE GULF WAR, 1990-1

Amphibious forces formed one part of the military response to Iraq's invasion of Kuwait on 2 August 1990. During the war, the USA maintained two marine brigades afloat. The 4th Marine Expeditionary Brigade (MEB) conducted 13 exercises and feints in the Gulf in the period between October and February. The 5th MEB arrived in January 1991. While some contingencies were developed for amphibious assaults against Iraqi lines of communication – for example, Operation Tiger, which planned for the deployment of a marine expeditionary force in the area between

Umm Qasr and al-Faw – amphibious forces acted in the main in a diversionary role. They tied down Iraqi troops on the coast and complicated Iraqi planning.

The passage of amphibious forces to the Gulf War battle zone was facilitated by two factors in particular. First, the transit times for key elements of the amphibious force were significantly reduced by the existence of pre-positioned equipment. Rather than having to move from the USA or Europe, parts of the amphibious force were already available at short notice, since three US Maritime Pre-Positioning Ships (MPS) were deployed at the island base of Diego Garcia. These MPSs were ordered to the Gulf on 7 August and arrived only a few days later. Each vessel was 755ft (230m) long and capable of moving in one load more than 3000 C-141 airlift flights. Also equipped for rapid offloading, the MPSs allowed the USA to fly more than 16,000 personnel of 7th Marine Expeditionary Brigade into the Gulf, picking up heavy equipment once they were there. Overall,

BELOW: The small aircraft carriers of the British *Invincible* class exploit the VSTOL ability of the Sea Harrier to provide the capabilities of an aircraft carrier in a relatively small hull. However, these ships can only embark a limited number of aircraft and the lack of fixed-wing airborne early warning aircraft proved a serious handicap during the 1982 Falklands conflict.

13 MPSs were deployed from Guam, Diego Garcia and the Atlantic, and brought the heavy equipment for three MEBs. In addition, the US Navy deployed 11 Afloat Pre-positioned Ships (APS). The APSs were ready-stocked with supplies, fuel and even field hospitals. For the Coalition force as a whole, roughly 95 per cent of the heavy equipment and supplies were moved by sea. The efforts of the MPSs and APSs were supplemented by specialist transport ships, such as the eight US SL-7 fast sealift vessels, and by the stock of reserve ships which had been provided by US Military Sealift Command.

A second factor which facilitated the passage of amphibious forces to the Gulf was Coalition command of the sea. Iraq's ability to challenge Coalition sea passage to the battle zone was limited at the best of times, given the short ranges of its available forces. The massive preponderance of Coalition air and maritime power further undermined Iraqi hopes of inflicting losses while Coalition forces were at sea. Iraq lacked the broad multi-layered defences to challenge Coalition sea control; it had no submarines or long-range surface attack aircraft and its only major surface vessel was the 1850-tonne *Ibn Khaldun*, which was in fact a training ship. Its remaining ships were essentially fast attack craft or minesweepers: six Osa

II and two or three Osa I guided-missile fast attack craft; three large SO-1 patrol craft; four or five Zhuk coastal patrol craft; two Soviet T-43; three *Yevgenya*-class ocean-going minesweepers; and three *Nestin*-class in-shore minesweepers. Even though it was augmented by a number of small captured Kuwaiti boats, this force was unable to threaten sea transit lanes. What little threat it did pose was removed when the Iraqi flotilla attempted to cross the Bubiyan channel between 28 and 29 August, and was caught and destroyed by Coalition helicopters and aircraft.

In contrast, Coalition maritime power was enormous. Not since World War II had such a large maritime force been collected together. The USA had more than 160 ships deployed to support the operation at its height, including six aircraft carriers. More than 60 ships were deployed by Allied nations, including the Gulf states, Argentina, Australia, Canada, Denmark, France, Italy, the Netherlands and the UK. In addition to performing counter-mining operations and providing Naval Gunfire Support (NGS) and support for the Coalition strategic bombing and defensive/offensive air campaigns, this force ensured that Coalition control of the sea remained virtually unchallenged. In the air, the story was similar. Iraq had no specialized naval intelligence planes, no maritime patrol and no specialized armed scout. Coalition air superiority, achieved through the overwhelming deployment of land and carrier-borne aircraft, largely negated the airborne missile threat from Iraq's airforce, which declined to contest air superiority and flew instead to Iran.

Coalition forces had to transit through several choke-points, not least the Suez canal, the Straits of Hormuz and the southern exit of the Red Sea. This could have been problematic if Iraq had had the advantage of local allies to exploit this vulnerability, or if Iraq had invaded Saudi Arabia, which would have given them airbases from which to attack forces moving through these areas. In the event, however, even those willing to give some political support to Iraq – for example Libya, Jordan and Yemen – were unwilling to provide military aid. In any case, of these three, only Libya possessed a meaningful ability to disrupt the transit of forces, since its sea-denial capabilities

included land-based air assets and submarines. Even if Iraq had taken bases in Saudi Arabia, it is questionable how long Iraqi aircraft would have been able to survive the challenge from Coalition air power.

In the Gulf War, then, the Coalition reaped the benefits of an uncontested passage to the Gulf battle zone. This was important politically as well as militarily. The likelihood of significant casualties en route would have greatly hampered the building of a domestic and international political consensus for the launch of a military operation in the first place. Militarily, although the Coalition's effective command of the sea – which had been achieved by building up a massive preponderance of maritime power – did not, in itself, guarantee victory, it was a major contributory factor. Uncontested transit enabled the accumulated forces to launch their crushing air and ground offensive.

BELOW: USNS *Regulus* and USNS *Trucker*. Both participated in the Desert Shield/Desert Storm operations. The concentration of equipment and supplies during transit is evident by the crowded deck in the foreground, and is one reason why amphibious forces are potentially so vulnerable during this phase.

ABOVE: The USNS *Suribachi* moving through the Suez Canal in August 1990. Choke-points like the Suez Canal can make the amphibious force vulnerable to attack. It may also create political difficulties to move forces through them.

CASE STUDY: THE FALKLANDS WAR, 1982

The Falklands war began after the seizure of the Falklands (Las Islas Malvinas) by Argentina on 2 April 1982. Operation Corporate, the UK's campaign to take back the islands, was the UK's largest amphibious operation since Suez in 1956. In this operation, the passage to the battle zone proved to be critical. UK forces had to shepherd an improvised task force of ships and men over 8000 miles (12,870km) through inhospitable seas against an adversary which had credible sea-denial capabilities. As Argentina reinforced its garrison on the Falklands to more than 10,000 men, it became clear that the UK's margin of superiority was very narrow indeed, and that the loss of forces en route might serve to render the whole operation both politically and materially untenable.

The journey to the Falklands battle zone offered a number of challenges to the British. The force contained many vulnerable STUFT ships. In addition, the forces organized to retake the island had been assembled very quickly, without the required planning, logistics and training efforts. Shortcomings before the sailing would thus have to be remedied en route. Futhermore, Argentina possessed significant air and naval assets that would be able to threaten the amphibious force. The Argentine Navy possessed three

seaworthy submarines and the surface fleet deployed five modern ships, namely two Type-42 destroyers and three corvettes, and six old ships: four Exocet armed destroyers, the cruiser *Belgrano*, and the small aircraft carrier *25 de Mayo*. Collectively, the Argentine Navy and Airforce could deploy more than 60 modern combat aircraft, including Exocet armed Super Entendards, capable of reaching the Falklands battle zone.

The first ships and submarines left Britain on 4 April. Argentina lacked the capability to contest the first portion of the British forces' passage due to the distance from the Argentine mainland. The UK was thus able to push forces in ad hoc groups to Ascension Island where elements of the fleet began to assemble and form into an Advance Guard of seven frigates and destroyers, an Amphibious Task Group, and a 'Carrier Battle Group', including the carriers *Illustrious* and *Hermes*. Both of the carriers were small, each ordinarily deploying air groups of six Sea Harrier Vertical/Short Take Off and Landing (VSTOL) jets and an equal number of helicopters, although more were embarked for the campaign. The long journey was put to good use, with frequent drills and training conducted between ships. Ascension Island, with its safe anchorage and 10,000ft (3048m) runway, would prove to be a vital British logistics base, and also provided an opportunity to redistribute cargoes that had been laden quickly and not necessarily tactically. The Amphibious Group left Ascension on 7 May, having been preceded by the other two groups.

British submarines effectively ended the Argentine surface threat. The nuclear-powered submarine HMS *Conqueror* sank the *Belgrano* on 2 May. Although this was politically controversial – the sinking took place 35 miles (56km) outside of a British-declared Total Exclusion Zone around the islands – the risk posed by British submarines kept the remainder of the Argentine surface fleet, including its carrier, in port. Despite many submarine scares that began almost as soon as the Carrier Group left Ascension, Argentine submarines also proved to be ineffective; one was destroyed, another suffered mechanical failure and no British ships were torpedoed. As a consequence of its NATO roles, the Royal Navy had a well-developed Anti-Submarine Warfare (ASW) capability.

Protecting the amphibious task force from air attack proved to be more difficult. The need to defend the approaching amphibious force had to be balanced against the risk of losing too many escorts or a carrier, which would jeopardize the campaign as a whole. The carriers were therefore deployed to the east of the Falklands, and not between the Falklands and the Argentine mainland, with a picket line of frigates and destroyers 20 miles (32km) in front. Despite the loss of some ships, including HMS *Sheffield*, and damage to several others, this deployment proved successful. Argentina failed to lengthen the runway at Port Stanley, so its fighter/strike aircraft had to fly from the mainland bases which were 380–420nm (703–78nkm) to the west, and could often spend no more than a few minutes in the vicinity of British ships. This – plus a number of other factors, including the skilful use of outnumbered but manoeuvrable Harrier VSTOL aircraft – meant that, although the Argentine forces bravely continued to contest control of the air around the Falklands, the combination of sub-marines, surface vessels and carrier air capabilities gave the UK sufficient sea control to allow the amphibious task force to rendezvous with the carrier group on 18 May and to allow it deploy

to the objective area. In addition, prior to the arrival of the amphibious force, the carrier group was able to carry out several preparatory activities against the Argentine Falklands garrison, including a blockade and air attacks.

Operation Corporate succeeded by a narrow margin, a success largely due to avoiding undue attrition to the amphibious force en route. It demonstrated that, although a long passage to the battle zone poses many challenges, it can also provide an opportunity to train, plan and resupply in preparation for the amphibious assault. It also demonstrated that sea control need not be total in order to successfully complete the passage to the battle zone; it need only be sufficient. However, it also highlighted the dangers involved in

BELOW: Marines embark from the liner *Canberra* during the Falklands war. STUFT may provide vital amphibious capacity, but, as this photo shows, they are not always ideal for complex evolutions such as transferring troops.

transiting through areas contested by a capable foe. It required the deployment of virtually the whole spectrum of Britain's conventional naval capabilities to ensure that the Amphibious Task Group reached the Falklands. Perhaps only small changes in Argentine strategy, such as preparing to base jets on the Falklands, might have decisively challenged the UK's control of the sea. The impact that the loss of sea control can have on the viability of amphibious operations is well illustrated by the battle of Midway.

CASE STUDY: MIDWAY, 1942

Although it is best known as a fierce and decisive carrier battle, the Japanese plan at Midway was built around an amphibious operation designed to attack and occupy Midway atoll. The Japanese hoped that the seizure of Midway would precipitate a major US counter-response as well as act as a catalyst for an air and surface engagement that would destroy the core of US Pacific maritime power.

The Japanese plan was an exceedingly complex one. The invasion of Midway itself was timed for 7 June 1942, as this was the last date when there would be sufficient moonlight to conduct amphibious operations, and the earliest date that forces previously in the Indian Ocean could be moved up and made ready. In addition to coordinating with forces that would engage in a diversionary attack on the Aleutian Islands, the Midway operation required cooperation between a number of different fleet elements. The Midway Invasion Fleet under Vice-Admiral

BELOW: The British carriers such as HMS *Hermes* were vital assets during the Falklands conflict and played a crucial role in protecting the British amphibious group as it advanced to the objective area.

Nobutake was divided into an amphibious group called the Midway Occupation Force, which had transports carrying 5000 men, a seaplane carrier, and an escort of destroyers, and the Second Fleet Main Body, which included four cruisers, two battleships and the light carrier *Zuiho*. Other elements included an Advance Force of 10 submarines, which was to establish a forward picket-line screening Pearl Harbor, the Midway Support Force of four cruisers and two destroyers under Vice Admiral Kurita, and a small Minesweeper Group. Second Fleet was to coordinate with Admiral Nagumo's I Carrier Striking Force formed around the aircraft carriers *Akagi*, *Kaga*, *Hiryu* and *Soryu*, which would sail from Japan to Midway, attacking the atoll on 4 June. Also from Japan would sail a separate Main Body consisting of three battleships (including the huge *Yamato*) with a destroyer escort. The various elements of the fleet advanced on a wide front in two main prongs: Second Fleet proceeded to the south-west of Midway, and the Main Body and I Carrier Strike force to the Northwest.

Critical to the success of the plan, which was codenamed Operation MI, was surprise. Admiral Yamamoto, the overall commander and the plan's architect, assumed that Japanese control of the seas around Midway would not be contested until after the landing. However, the USA had already broken JN25, the Japanese Navy's operational

code, and US knowledge of the Japanese plans had a range of implications: the US Pacific Fleet's main elements, Task Force 16 and Task Force 17, containing the carriers *Lexington*, *Hornet* and *Yorktown*, were already moving into position to conduct a quick, heavy attack; the Aleutian diversionary operation begun on 3 June did not succeed in diverting substantial US forces; the Japanese submarine screen had been passed even before it was deployed; and the defences of Midway were alert, and engaged in wide-ranging patrols with their Catalina PBY patrol aircraft.

The Midway invasion force was thus spotted on 3 June by a PBY aircraft from Midway, at a distance of 600 miles (965km) from the atoll, with Nagumo's carriers found soon after. Rear-Admiral Fletcher, commanding the US carrier striking force, turned the two US Task Forces south to a point around 200 miles (320km) north of Midway and prepared to launch his attack against the Japanese carriers early the next day. In doing so, Fletcher recognized that the outcome of the Japanese operation against Midway depended not upon the progress of the Midway Occupation Force but on the carriers providing it with protection. Without the air support to ensure sufficient sea control, the amphibious operation would be fatally compromised.

On 4 June, TF16 and TF17 began air attacks against Nagumo's carriers. Fortuitously for Fletcher, and reflecting

ABOVE: The two Japanese battleships *Yamato* (seen here) and *Mushashi* were the largest, most powerful battleships ever built. Armed with nine 18in (457mm) guns and an armour belt 16in (406mm) thick, they were a match for any other surface vessel. However, both were lost to massive air attacks.

the Japanese belief that US carriers were far from the area, Nagumo's force was caught while in the process of 'softening up' Midway with air attacks. While the attacking US aircraft – in particular the torpedo bombers – suffered heavily, the *Kaga*, *Akagi*, *Soryu* and *Hiryu* were hit in succession and turned into blazing hulks. The successful Japanese counter-strikes against the *Yorktown* proved to be small compensation for the destruction of Japan's carrier force.

At 0255 hours on 5 June, Yamamoto gave the orders for a general retreat. For the amphibious task force, the battle itself had been relatively uneventful; air attacks from Midway, including a force of B-17s, scored one hit on a Japanese oiler, but the damage was soon repaired. Yet the destruction of the core of I Carrier Striking Force was far more serious, and rendered the amphibious operation untenable. The likely fate of the Midway Occupation Force was indicated by Kurita's supporting force of heavy cruisers which, in a rather chaotic

withdrawal from the Midway area, was attacked by aircraft, with the *Mikuma* sunk and the *Mogami* heavily damaged.

Thus, it is clear that the main reason for the failure of the amphibious operation was the Japanese inability to secure sea control before the amphibious task group reached Midway. The Japanese assumption that Operation MI would catch the USA by surprise led them to believe that their amphibious forces would be able to transit to the Midway atoll before any US counter-response could take shape. In reality, however, the US forces were already placed to contest control of the Midway area and so the Imperial Navy's carrier force was caught providing support for the operations against Midway itself, instead of preparing to fight a carrier battle. The subsequent loss of more than half of Japanese fleet-carrier strength and the decimation of irreplaceable experienced air crews ceded the initiative to the USA in the Pacific. Being unable to ensure a secure passage during the long transit stages of Pacific

BELOW: The approach to Midway, 26 May to 5 June 1942. The Japanese plan at Midway was extremely complex. The amphibious operation itself was only one part of a grander move to lure the US Pacific Fleet into a decisive battle.

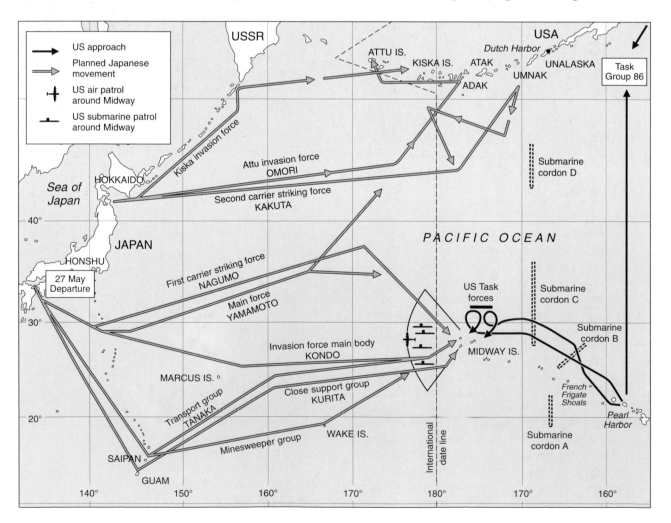

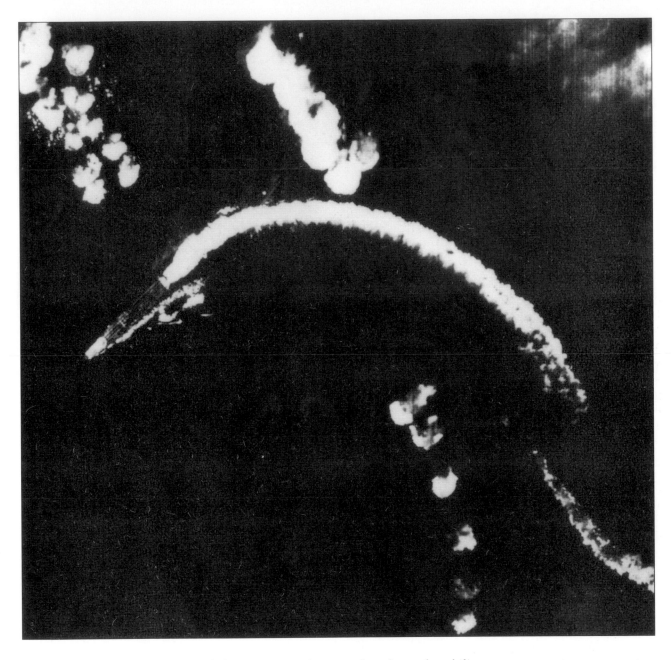

naval operations, Japan's amphibious capability was fatally undermined.

CONCLUSION

Amphibious operations only have the opportunity to be successful if they can first get to the amphibious operations area. Whether and how an amphibious task force reaches the battle zone is thus a vital consideration for the commanders of the operation. It is important to understand the relationship between sea control and amphibious operations. Sea control is not an end in itself; in order for it to be useful, it needs to be exploited, and an important means of doing this is through amphibious operations. However, all successful amphibious

operations are based on the ability to achieve sufficient sea control and protect the amphibious forces from enemy attack. Command of the sea during the Gulf War gave the Coalition extraordinary military flexibility. During the Falklands war, by contrast, while the covering naval forces were able to ensure enough sea control to allow the amphibious force to move into position, it was a close-run affair. Had the Carrier Battle Group been badly damaged, and the British ceded air superiority, then the likely outcome would have been similar to Midway, where the damage inflicted on supporting carrier forces meant that the Japanese amphibious operation failed even before it reached the beach.

ABOVE: The Japanese carrier *Akagi* turns desperately to avoid attack from US aircraft. With the loss of its carrier force protection, the Midway amphibious operation was rendered untenable.

CHAPTER THREE

PRE-LANDING OPERATIONS

Preliminary operations can often increase the chances of success in amphibious assaults. Yet there are dilemmas involved in their use.

Pre-landing operations aim to create the best possible circumstances for the actual landing by isolating the objective area from sources of help, obtaining information that will help inform the plan of assault and preparing the objective area by degrading enemy defences. Pre-landing operations are an example of what is often termed 'shaping the littoral battlespace'. The littoral area is the region lying along or adjacent to the shore and therefore the term 'littoral battlespace' describes both the area of sea to be controlled in order to support operations ashore, and the area ashore to be supported and defended directly from the sea. Shaping the most advantageous situation on or below the surface of the sea and in the air, land, underwater and electro-magnetic dimensions of the littoral battle-space is vital in mounting a successful amphibious operation. The range of operations that may be undertaken in this sort of preparation is wide. Although most often associated with naval gunfire support (NGS), such as the huge barrages that pounded the Japanese defences of Iwo Jima, the pre-assault phase can also include deception, reconnaissance, mine counter-measures, airstrikes, underwater demolition, destruction of beach obstacles and special forces raids.

LEFT: The USS *West Virginia* fires 16-in (406-mm) salvoes onto Iwo Jima on 19 February 1945. Although often an impressive sight, Naval Gunfire Support (NGS) can be difficult to make effective. Despite the pre-landing bombardment, the US Marines met savage resistance to their landings at Iwo Jima.

Pre-assault operations are conducted in the objective area by subordinate elements of the amphibious task force. Often these tasks will be performed by a designated Advance Force. This advance force may begin conducting operations days or weeks prior to the arrival of the amphibious force. Although the forces used, the area of operation and the timescales may vary, both supporting operations and pre-assault operations can involve similar tasks. Pre-landing operations can include work in many different areas.

THE DECEPTION AND DESTRUCTION OF THE ENEMY

Supporting operations can contribute to strategic deception. This is achieved by misleading the enemy as to the general area of attack. For example, in early 1943, as part of Operation Mincemeat, the submarine HMS *Seraph* dropped a dead body off the coast of Spain upon which were planted false plans for an Allied assault in the eastern Mediterranean. The Spanish picked up the body and the plans, and passed the latter on to the Germans. The false plans obscured the real target of the intended Allied landings (which was, in fact, Sicily). Pre-assault operations can also be used to create operational and tactical surprise. Advance forces may conduct ruses to obscure the exact landing site through demonstrations or covert landings. For example, prior to the Inchon landings in 1950, covert forces were sent ashore to a beach south of Inchon on 12 and 13 September to plant decoy reconnaissance equipment. This equipment was found by enemy patrols and misled the North Koreans about the landing point.

In a process that is commonly called 'destruction and neutralization of distant forces', supporting attacks can be made on forces some way from the intended Amphibious Operation Area, such as submarine bases, logistic centres and airbases. Such attacks may contribute to deception operations but they can also be used to prevent the enemy from bringing up reinforcements, to disrupt the enemy's higher command and control capabilities or to neutralize forces that could intervene later against the landing or subsequent operations. Prior to the Japanese landings in the Philippines at

ABOVE: UH-60 Blackhawk helicopters land US troops on the island of Grenada during Operation Urgent Fury. The need for surprise meant pre-landing operations were kept to a minimum.

TOP RIGHT: Bombing played a vital role in deceiving the Germans as to the intended landing points of the Allied invasion of France. Here, US Marauders return over the west coast of France having attacked targets at Cherbourg.

BOTTOM RIGHT: In addition to reconnaissance of the beach areas, diving teams can mark and/or destroy enemy beach defences.

Pre-landing operations can be divided into two general types: supporting operations and pre-assault operations. Supporting operations are pre-landing tasks carried out by forces that are not part of the amphibious task force. They are often carried out before any part of the force has arrived in the objective area, but can also be conducted in parallel with the deployment into the objective area. Supporting operations may even be carried out in completely different theatres of operation.

The command and control of such supporting operations will usually be conducted at a level higher than the amphibious commander. Supporting operations can be carried out by a wide variety of forces, ranging from land-based strategic bombers through surface action groups to irregular forces that are operating behind enemy lines.

Davao and Batan, for example, Japanese land-based aircraft from Formosa attacked US bases on the Philippine islands in order to create disruption and confusion, and to limit the ability of US forces to respond to the landings.

MORALE AND INTELLIGENCE

Using psychological warfare, supporting and pre-assault operations can perform operations which are designed to reduce the enemy's will to resist. These tasks may include media broadcasts or dropping leaflets on enemy troops. Both of these activities were used against Iraqi forces in the Gulf War in order to undermine their morale. Prior to the US attack on Saipan on 15 June 1944, US aircraft were used to drop leaflets urging the Japanese defenders to surrender.

Supporting operations can also play the important pre-landing role of obtaining intelligence on the objective area. This is achieved through photo reconnaissance by aircraft and submarines, the activities of friendly agents or irregular forces, electronic intercepts and direction-finding and the monitoring of remote sensors. Pre-assault operations will often gather intelligence on local conditions through such tasks as detailed hydrographic surveys of beaches and the scouting of potential helicopter landing zones. Meteorological and oceanographic information on local weather conditions and information such as beach gradients, obstacles, tides and so on may have an important bearing on vital issues, such as when and where to conduct the landing. For example, prior to the US assault on Tarawa in November 1943, major pre-landing intelligence efforts were made: aerial photographs were taken by land- and carrier-based aircraft, and the submarine *Nautilus* made an 18-day reconnaissance of potential landing beaches, taking 2000 periscope photographs during that period. Nevertheless, mistaken calculations about the water clearance over the surrounding reefs meant that many of the assaulting landing craft were stranded some way from shore and heavy casualties were taken by the attacking forces.

ISOLATION OF THE ENEMY

Pre-landing operations may also be employed in order to isolate the intended

ABOVE: Ordnance men load a 500lb (227kg) bomb onto an SBD Bomber on USS *Enterprise*, during the Guadalcanal landings on 7 August 1942. The aircraft carrier's combination of reconnaissance, defensive air, and offensive capabilities can provide a decisive advantage during landings and may be vital if the amphibious operation is conducted beyond the range of friendly land-based aircraft.

TOP RIGHT: US Navy SEALs were landed prior to the assault on Grenada. The risks associated with such covert insertion operations are high.

BOTTOM RIGHT: Sea King helicopters (top right) on HMS *Hermes* are re-armed with torpedoes during the Falklands war. Torpedo-armed Sea Kings were part of the British Anti-Submarine Warfare (ASW) effort.

amphibious objective from nearby sources of support. Attacks by aircraft, NGS, submarines, amphibious raiding forces and so on can be targeted against enemy airfields, aircraft, communications, supplies, shipping and other targets. A core component of achieving enemy isolation is achieving and maintaining local air superiority. Carrier and land-based aircraft can isolate and neutralize the enemy and conduct Combat Air Patrols (CAPs) to achieve air superiority and suppress enemy air defences. Air superiority is usually vital for the success of amphibious operations; only 14 per cent of modern amphibious operations have succeeded where local air superiority has not been attained.

CONTROL OF THE SEA

Supporting maritime forces must establish sea control near to and within the amphibious objective area (AOA) before the amphibious assault can commence. Maintaining sea control within this more limited area, sometimes called 'precision sea control', can become particularly difficult if the enemy has sophisticated sea-denial capabilities. Coastal geography can obscure the

amphibious tasks force's sensors. Defence systems designed to exploit peculiar inshore conditions might be brought into play, including diesel submarines, short-range ground attack aircraft, fast patrol boats, mines and shore-based gun batteries and missile sites. While the choice of amphibious objective area should ideally take into account sea-control considerations, factors such as time, weather and geography can dictate an objective area where precision sea control may be a challenging task. Precision sea control will often require establishing a defence in depth, cooperating – wherever possible – with supporting air, surface and subsurface groups to achieve sufficient battlespace dominance. It will often require efforts to prepare the sea within the objective area through mine clearance, hydrographic surveys and laying anti-submarine nets.

Pre-landing operations may also embody destruction and harassment tasks in order to suppress or destroy specific enemy defences or simply to confuse and impede the enemy's general defensive efforts. Airstrikes, NGS, precision guided munitions attack (for example, submarine-based Cruise missiles), raids

ABOVE: Royal Marines Special Boat Squadron (SBS) personnel. Special forces are often used in advance of amphibious operations. They can perform reconnaissance tasks and can also be used to sabotage and disrupt enemy forces further inland.

and clandestine operations can all be used to degrade enemy defences and ensure the success of an amphibious landing. Potential targets can include beach- and landing-zone defences, enemy gun emplacements, command posts, observation posts and airfields. Against Iwo Jima, for example, supporting operations by US Air Force B-24 and B-25 bombers involved bombardment of the islands for 74 days before the actual assault. Prior to the Inchon landings, the North Korean defences were subjected to two days of air and gunfire attack.

Prior to the landing, it may also be expedient to begin the clearance or marking of natural or man-made beach obstacles. Often frogmen are employed to carry out these tasks. Organized into Underwater Demolition Teams (UDTs), frogmen were used by the USA at Iwo Jima in order to survey and clear the offshore area of obstacles.

Supporting and pre-assault operations may also involve smaller landings, tasked

with reconnaissance of landing zones or drop zones, the destruction of specific targets or the harassment of the enemy. Often, such landings are used to capture offshore islands for use as artillery sites, navigation aids or logistic points. Prior to the Inchon landings, subsidiary assaults were made on the islands of Tokchok-Do and Yonghung-Do on 17 and 20 August. Occupation of these islands helped to ensure passage through Flying Fish channel into Inchon harbour itself. As part of Operation Anvil of 15 August 1944 – the Allies' landing in southern France – a preliminary landing was made by Allied troops who set up roadblocks on coastal and inland roads which were designed to cause severe chaos in the German rear areas.

Finally, supporting and pre-assault operations can include 'covert insertions'. The focus of these operations is to minimize the risk to the landing force by inserting facilitating forces to coordinate the movement of the landing forces and the delivery of supporting firepower, and also to gather local intelligence relevant to the landing plan. This may involve the deployment of observers to spot for artillery and NGS support, or to coordinate tactical air support for the landings. It may also include engineer reconnaissance troops who will identify and perhaps also begin to clear any defensive obstacles.

DIFFICULTIES OF PRE-LANDING OPERATIONS

Pre-landing operations have often made a valuable contribution to the success of amphibious operations. However, it should not be assumed that they are universally useful; often the choice of their type, scale and nature can be difficult. The need for speed may constrain the scope of preliminary operations: many Soviet operations in World War II were organized very quickly and opportunities for pre-landing operations were often limited. Capability provides other opportunities or constraints: the lack of guns may undermine the likely effectiveness of Naval Gunfire Support (NGS); a vertical envelopment capability may make beach preparation less important. One clear dilemma is how to strike the balance between preparation and surprise, especially where the use of an advance force is concerned. As far as possible, pre-landing operations should not compromise the intended place or time of the main landing. At Saipan, the pattern of preparatory bombing and leafleting led the Japanese commander to correctly guess the enemy landing beach despite US diversionary efforts. Another difficulty is posed by the nature of the enemy defences; different defensive configurations may make some pre-landing operations more useful than others. With a forward defence of the beach, an emphasis on preparation and destruction operations may be required. Where the beach is lightly defended and the main defenders are in reserve, the emphasis may have to be on isolation and interdiction of the beach area. Command and control can also pose challenges. The fact that supporting operations may be conducted by forces which are not part of the amphibious force can create coordination and sequencing problems between the amphibious forces and supporting forces. At Gallipoli, for example, a separate naval attack in November 1914 made to determine the effectiveness of naval gunfire on the Turkish forts warned the defenders that a

LEFT: British Royal Marines move towards the shore in light raiding craft known as 'Rigid Raiders'. The speed and low profile of these craft make them ideal for raiding operations. They can also be carried by helicopter.

RIGHT: The SBS in training, post-World War II. High levels of proficiency are required by such forces if pre-landing insertions are to be effective. The discovery and/or capture of personnel engaged in covert operations may alert the enemy to the chosen landing area.

military effort might be made against the Straits so that, when the first phase of the Gallipoli attack was launched in February 1915, the defences had been improved. Political restrictions relating to legitimacy, risk and the infliction of casualties may constrain the choice of available preliminary activities, especially in limited wars or low-intensity operations. US Marines went ashore in Somalia in 1992 against beaches 'defended' by television crews and, in the Lebanon in 1958, onto beaches occupied by local sunbathers and ice-cream vendors. Concern for civilian casualties, the risk to friendly forces and international opinion can impose restrictive Rules of Engagement (ROE) that limit the potential scope for pre-landing operations such as destruction and isolation of beach areas.

Ultimately, then, while pre-landing operations can be very useful, they need to be tailored to specific conditions, such as the following: the capabilities of the friendly forces; the capabilities and deployment of the enemy; the relative importance of surprise; any political considerations; and so on.

CASE STUDY: GRENADA, 1983

Operation Urgent Fury was launched on 25 October 1983 in response to political unrest on Grenada following the murder of the Prime Minister, Maurice Bishop. On 23 October, the Organization of Eastern Caribbean States (OECS) formally requested US assistance and, with 1000 US citizens on the island, including many students, the US agreed to help. The ATF consisted of five amphibious ships carrying the 22nd Marine Amphibious Unit (MAU), which had been diverted from the Mediterranean. The Operation Warning Order tasked the amphibious force to 'conduct military operations to protect and evacuate US and designated foreign nationals from Grenada, to neutralize Grenadan forces, stabilize the internal situation and maintain the peace ... and with OECS/friendly government participation, assist in the restoration of a democratic government on Grenada.'

Grenada was a 'no plan low-intensity conflict'. The choice of pre-landing operations was shaped by a number of considerations. One was the speed with which it had to be conducted. Initial planning for the operation began on 13 October and the 22nd MAU received its orders on 20 October. A prompt response was seen as essential to fulfil the mission's objectives and so the time available for preparatory operations was extremely limited. This was despite serious shortcomings in vital areas such as intelligence. The unit had no maps except a 1936 British navigation chart, no intelligence on the threat (estimates put the number of Cubans at 50–60, whereas there were 600 or more), or the number and location of evacuees. While preparatory operations might have remedied this deficiency, it was felt that the time factor militated against any time-consuming reconnaissance and intelligence operations. Furthermore, another consideration was operational security. Strategic surprise was lost when the Cuban Government learnt that the OECS had asked the USA to intervene. However, tactical surprise was still a possibility – this is why the initial plan was for a night attack – but this might have been compromised by sending supporting or advance forces to conduct preliminary operations. Maintaining secrecy was seen as vital in order to ensure the safety of the students. Another consideration was to minimize the number of casualties. Maintaining

operational security was central to the success of forcible entry by the US forces with minimum casualties. By maintaining surprise in this manner, no deception operations would be required. Also of concern was ensuring as little 'collateral damage' as possible. The task force's rules of engagement included directions to 'minimize the disruptive influence of military operations on the local economy commensurate with the accomplishment of the mission' and to 'execute initial tasks readily with the minimum damage and casualties'. This directed the US force away from preparatory activities such as naval gunfire or air attack. The potential dangers of these sorts of operations were illustrated when, during the assault itself, an airstrike was brought down on a suspected Grenadan Command Post. The post was destroyed, but so was a psychiatric hospital next to the fort, not shown on US maps. Another factor was the assessment of enemy capabilities; these the USA underestimated. It was not expected that there would be any significant opposition from the 50 or so Cuban military advisors or the 1200–1500-strong Grenadan military, thus further reducing the perceived need for prior operations to the landing. As it transpired, however, there were also 600 or more Cuban construction workers on the island, the majority of whom had had

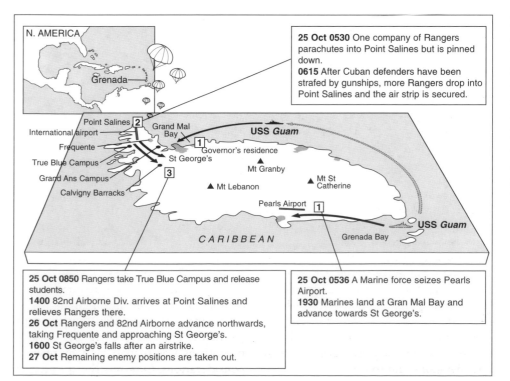

25 Oct 0530 One company of Rangers parachutes into Point Salines but is pinned down.
0615 After Cuban defenders have been strafed by gunships, more Rangers drop into Point Salines and the air strip is secured.

25 Oct 0850 Rangers take True Blue Campus and release students.
1400 82nd Airborne Div. arrives at Point Salines and relieves Rangers there.
26 Oct Rangers and 82nd Airborne advance northwards, taking Frequente and approaching St George's.
1600 St George's falls after an airstrike.
27 Oct Remaining enemy positions are taken out.

25 Oct 0536 A Marine force seizes Pearls Airport.
1930 Marines land at Gran Mal Bay and advance towards St George's.

LEFT: Operation Urgent Fury: a 'no plan low-intensity conflict'. The initial US plan for a beach landing on Grenada was cancelled when reconnaissance showed that the beaches were unsuitable. Instead US forces took the island through vertical envelopment and airborne landings, with amphibious landings following on.

ABOVE: Troops of the 82nd Airborne Division in Grenada. The 82nd followed up early on D-Day, landing in the south of the island in the Salines-True Blue-Calivigny area.

military training, as well as a number of anti-aircraft guns that were put to good use by the defenders. A final consideration was that of friendly capabilities. Less than 30 hours before the landing, the ATF was told that elements of the Army Rangers and 82nd Airborne would also be involved. Although this did create some command and control difficulties, it further tipped the balance of forces in favour of the USA.

The outcome of these considerations was that Operation Urgent Fury was launched with relatively few pre-landing operations. It was hoped that a surprise, simultaneous attack against key targets would quickly overwhelm the defenders. Those activities that were conducted proved both the utility and the difficulty of such operations.

Four elements were involved in the operation: TF121 (Airborne Task Force); TF 123 (Rangers); TF 124 (Amphibious Task Force); and TF 126 (Air Force). The plan was that during the morning darkness on 25 October Marines would land and take the northern part of the island, including Pearls Airport. The Rangers were tasked with taking the southern part of the island, including the medical school campus containing the US students, and a new airport that was under construction at Point Salines. Navy 'SEALs' (Sea, Air, Land Special Forces) would then move into the capital, capture the radio station, free political prisoners and release the Governor-General. Paratroops would then be brought in to mop up and to provide secure entry for a

350-man Caribbean peace-keeping force.

Members of the Barbados Defence Force had already obtained intelligence while on the island, but US officials did not pass it on to the assault forces. On the evening of the 23rd, navigation beacon teams were sent to Point Salines airport to install navigation beacons for guiding in airborne forces. However, the night drop went wrong and several men drowned. Another attempt was made on 24 October, but this also failed; in the mean time, the delays in mounting the operation as a whole put back the landing until 0500 hours, when it would be light, thus rendering the navigation beacons unnecessary. Of rather more use was information from the island's beaches provided by two SEAL groups scouting there. While one group was lost, the other reported at 0200 hours on 15 October that the proposed landing beach was obstructed. At that point, it was decided to launch the assault by helicopter alone. The first group was flown off at 0315 hours.

The nature of the pre-landing operations for Urgent Fury well illustrate the competing pressures of preparation and surprise on a commander. The imperative to provide a rapid solution to the crisis and assumptions about the capabilities of the enemy directed the operation's commander towards sparse pre-landing operations. They focused on covert insertions for the smooth ingress of the US forces. Even these limited operations proved to be difficult to complete; nevertheless, as the SEALs identified the unsuitability of the proposed amphibious landing site, they prevented a potential débâcle at the water's edge.

CASE STUDY: FALKLANDS WAR, 1982
The initial amphibious assault at San Carlos provides a good example of the possible roles of pre-landing operations in a high-intensity war. The nature of the operations was shaped by a number of factors. One was the imminent onset of winter, the arrival of which would signal the end of the amphibious effort, if a landing had not already been effected; this placed a limit on the potential for preparation. Another was the balance of forces. The Falklands were defended by three Argentine infantry brigades, a

marine battalion, two artillery groups with 4.1in (105mm) howitzers, and two squadrons of armoured cars for a total of about 13,000 men. The Falklands garrison also had 19 helicopters, about 20 light attack aircraft, and supporting land-based aircraft on the Argentine mainland 400 miles (644km) to the west. The British forces available for the initial landing were much smaller; three Commando brigades and two battalions of the Parachute Regiment. Including special forces from the SAS and SBS, the British landing force could muster 5500 men. Capability gaps in the British force also had to be taken into consideration – such as its comparatively weak Naval Gunfire Support ability – as well as the potentially fatal consequences for the campaign as a whole of substantial losses amongst the maritime elements of the task force during a landing. The British plan therefore accorded a central place to deception and surprise. The British possessed one important advantage: detailed intelligence on the coastal geography of the islands, provided by a survey conducted by Royal Marines officer Ewen Southby-Tailyour just prior to the war.

Strategic surprise was not possible because Argentina knew the destination of the British task force. Tactical surprise, however, was possible. The Falkland Islands had 2500 miles (4020km) of coastline with 30 beaches suitable for landings. Understandably unwilling to spread his forces out, the Argentine

commander created a strong static defence around Port Stanley, the capital. Smaller forces were distributed around the island at places such as Goose Green and Pebble Island. British pre-landing operations were therefore directed towards the need to undermine the capabilities of the defence, to establish sufficient sea control for a landing, and to deceive the enemy about the landing place so that it would be, as far as possible, unopposed.

The main pre-landing operations were pre-assault tasks. They were performed by an advance force, consisting of a 'Carrier Battle Group' of two small carriers, with around 20 Harrier jets each, and their escorts. When this force arrived off the Falklands on 29 April it instituted a

ABOVE: The deck of USS *Guam*. An assault ship, rather than an aircraft carrier, the USS *Guam* is designed to provide support and transport for its embarked Marine unit. In Grenada, its helicopter assets were a core component in the assault plan.

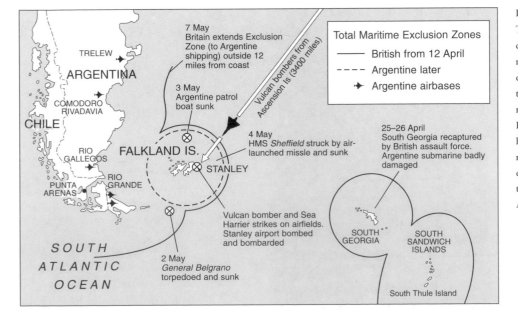

LEFT: The Falklands war. The eventual British success depended in no small measure on military operations conducted before the amphibious task force reached San Carlos. Preliminary operations helped to secure the necessary measure of sea control as well as attacking the logistics and morale of Argentine forces.

ABOVE: A Harrier prepares for launch from the deck of HMS *Hermes* during the Falklands war. Without the small carriers *Invincible* and *Hermes*, the British attempt to retake the Falklands would almost inevitably have failed; indeed, it would probably not have been undertaken in the first place.

BELOW: HMS *Ardent* sinks in San Carlos Water, 22 May 1982, having been bombed by Argentine aircraft. Even with the protection provided by British aircraft and the distance from the Argentine airbases, enemy air attack posed a very dangerous challenge to British amphibious operations.

blockade, preventing major reinforcement of the Argentine forces by sea or air and beginning the process of undermining Argentine morale and logistics. This also contributed towards the isolation of the intended landing beach at San Carlos, as it encouraged the deployment of Argentine forces closer to their logistics base at Port Stanley. At the same time, the advance force established air cover for the subsequent landing operations, flying a continuous Combat Air Patrol (CAP) that also impeded Argentine efforts at reconnaissance. The British plan was to land at San Carlos Bay on the opposite side of the island to Port Stanley. To do this, the amphibious task force would have to move into Falkland Sound, the straits between West and East Falkland Islands. Argentina already believed that San Carlos was an unlikely landing spot because of the lack of sea room to manoeuvre and also because it was so far from Port Stanley. British pre-landing operations were designed to reinforce the

perception that Port Stanley was the only choice of landing site. At 0340 hours on 1 May a total of 21 bombs, each weighing 1000lb (453kg), were dropped on Port Stanley airfield from an RAF Vulcan bomber after a 3730-mile (6000km) flight from Ascension Island, and later in the day, Harrier attacks were also directed against the airfield. With Argentine attention focused on Port Stanley, air attacks were reinforced by naval gunfire from British ships; it was hoped this would give the impression of 'softening-up' attacks. The British media also played a role in diversionary operations, stating in war reportage that the only landing operation being considered was against Port Stanley.

In preparation for the main assault, Special Forces began to land in order to collect information and to attack outlying Argentine positions. On 15 May, 44 SAS landed on Pebble Island at the northern end of Falkland Sound. These attacked the garrison and destroyed 11 aircraft before withdrawing. An eight-man SAS team was also inserted into Argentina to report on air operations from the mainland. One important concern was that the Sound might be mined, since the British had no minesweepers at the time of the landing. So, on 10 and 11 May, the frigate *Alacrity* was sent to investigate whether any mines were present. It determined that there were no mines, but also alerted a small Argentine force based near San Carlos, who sent a small detachment to an outpost that over-looked the northern entrance to the Sound and past which amphibious ships would have to transit.

The amphibious task force, with two assault ships, six logistic landing ships and a large number of STUFT, joined the carrier force on 18 May. On the night of 20/21 May transports began to enter Falklands Sound. In the event, tactical surprise was complete. No NGS or air attack was used to prepare the San Carlos landing. Instead, prior to the landing, a section of the SBS were sent ashore to deal with the enemy observation post. On D-Day, 22 May, the attack itself was launched quietly onto San Carlos; all the troops were ashore in four hours. Precision sea control was conducted by escorts, with one frigate remaining with the amphibious shipping and five frigates

and a destroyer forming a line at the entrance to the sound. In addition, the carriers maintained a Combat Air Patrol. The Argentine Airforce commenced heavy attacks on the British the following day, but the amphibious force had succeeded in getting its troops ashore.

Pre-landing operations thus played a critical role in the success of the San Carlos landings. A combination of supporting operations and pre-assault operations were central to creating the deception necessary for an unopposed landing. The weight of air and NGS bombardment was used where the landing was not, in order to conceal the intentions of the British. Without these operations, the vulnerable amphibious force may have faced significant opposition, especially from the air, the consequences of which were clear from the later heavy losses suffered at Fitzroy and Bluff Cove.

CASE STUDY: OPERATION OVERLORD

Operation Overlord provides an example of pre-landing operations against a heavily defended shoreline. The allied invasion of Normandy on 6 June 1944 was the largest amphibious invasion in history, and pre-assault operations played an important part in the overall success of the landings. Under the command of Field Marshal Rommel, the defences facing the invasion were formidable. Forced to compromise between, on the one hand, defending forward and defeating an invasion in the water and, on the other, maintaining forces in reserve to counter-attack, the Germans had built up several layers of defence. Although lacking troops, there were four successive belts of offshore obstacles extending seawards and the landing area was strewn with obstacles and explosive devices. Engineers had constructed anti-tank walls, ditches and gun emplacements. Rommel also had control of three Panzer divisions for counter-attacks. Other forces available included 3rd Air Fleet with around 500 operational aircraft, and the German Navy could provide a small number of destroyers, torpedo boats and fast-attack craft, as well as 17 submarines. Moreover, the Germans were expecting an attack in 1944, the consensus being that it would take place in May.

Pre-landing operations were conducted extensively. Major efforts were made at intelligence-gathering to enable the Allies to develop as complete a picture of the enemy defences as possible. Use was made of aerial reconnaissance, Ultra intercepts, and intelligence from agents and the French Resistance. Covert landings were conducted well before the landings to engage in beach reconnaissance. These intelligence efforts gave the Allies a good picture of the Atlantic Wall and the troops manning it. On the contrary, the Germans were blinded by a massive Allied counter-intelligence effort. Through the use of

ABOVE: A low-level RAF reconnaissance photo of beach defences at Normandy. These obstacles were covered at high tide and were designed to rip the bottom from enemy landing vessels.

ABOVE: HMS *Roberts* providing NGS for the Normandy landings. This ship was one of four specialist monitors deployed by the Royal Navy. They were designed specifically for shore bombardment, with a main armament of two 15in (381mm) and eight 4in (102mm) guns.

spurious radio communications and the building of dummy encampments, the Allies convinced the Germans of the existence of First US Army Group (FUSAG) located opposite the Pas de Calais. This entirely fictitious formation reinforced the German belief that the attack, when it came, would not be in Normandy. Even when Overlord was launched, Hitler remained convinced for a time that it was merely a feint. The isolation of the Normandy area was carried out by US and British heavy bombers which began pounding transportation targets. From February to June 1944, the US 8th and 9th Airforces and Britain's 2nd Tactical Airforce dropped nearly 80,000 tonnes of bombs on 80 rail and road targets, including rail junctions, river crossings and depots. These served to hamper the movement of German reinforcements, although the bombing caused significant collateral damage, inflicting 12,000 French and Belgian casualties. Air attacks on these targets were stepped up in the period immediately preceding D-Day. They also helped to bring out German fighter strength, the attrition of which contributed to strengthening Allied

superiority for the Overlord operation. Pre-landing bombardments were conducted by ships and aircraft. NGS was delivered by seven battleships, 23 cruisers and numerous destroyers. Rocket batteries mounted on landing craft were used. The bombardment of the beach defences was kept short in the interests of surprise; it had a mixed effect, with the weather interfering in some of the air operations, for example the planned bombing of Omaha beach. While the bombardment succeeded in suppressing many of the defenders, it destroyed only 14 per cent of the emplaced guns.

Precision sea control was undertaken as part of Operation Overlord. The aim was to neutralize enemy threats to the invasion fleet by blocking both ends of the English Channel with maritime forces. Three hundred Allied minesweepers were used to prepare the approaches to the beaches. However, many mines survived and a total of 43 ships were sunk or damaged during the operation. Maritime forces also engaged in aggressive anti-submarine warfare in an effort to neutralize this dangerous threat. In this, the Allies had great success: by 30 June, only four out of 25 U-boats ordered forward by Germany had reached the amphibious area. Luftwaffe efforts to attack the fleet were also beaten off, with only one destroyer sunk. Some sorties were launched by German surface forces, but these were disrupted by bad weather and Allied air superiority.

Many other pre-landing operations were used. Harassing operations were conducted by the French Resistance. In preparation for the landing, electronic counter-measures were undertaken, including the destruction of some German radar installations, and the blinding of others. Some beach clearance was undertaken; Overlord saw the first use by the British of UDTs, or LCOCUs (Landing Craft Obstacle Clearance Units), as they were termed. Two Midget submarines spent 5 June offshore on the sea bottom. At 0500 hours on 6 June they surfaced just off the invasion beach and erected special telescoping masts with seaward flashing lights to guide in the first landing ships.

The range of pre-landing operations undertaken for Overlord was thus broad. Intelligence operations played a vital part in informing the development of the amphibious plans. Deception operations helped to achieve surprise and to encourage the Germans to focus their defensive efforts away from Normandy. Interdiction operations helped to slow the movement of German reinforcements once the landings were under way. Given how slim the margin of error was on 6 June, it is clear that effective preparatory operations were a necessary precursor for Allied success.

CONCLUSION

Favourably shaping the littoral battle-space, in all its dimensions, is not something that should necessarily be left to the assault itself. The risk and complexity of an amphibious assault require the commander to think carefully about how the objective area can be prepared before the landing starts. Yet the choice of preparatory operations needs to be carefully made. Considerations such as the relative benefits of surprise, the availability of time, capabilities, and the distribution of enemy forces need to be weighed up if pre-landing operations are to make a positive contribution to the outcome of an amphibious assault.

BELOW: US DUKWs carry troops and equipment to the Normandy beaches. The DUKW, or 'Duck', was a 2-tonne 6x6 amphibious truck that could carry 25 troops or 5000lb (2268kg) of cargo. While it had more land mobility than the US LVT, it lacked armour.

CHAPTER FOUR

SECURING THE BEACH

Unopposed landings can be problematic, but opposed landings are amongst the most difficult and dangerous of all military operations.

The effective preparation, assembly and passage of forces to the objective area can contribute significantly to the success of amphibious operations. However, they cannot guarantee a favourable outcome. Ultimately, these preparatory stages are only a precursor to the main event: the actual securing of the beach through an amphibious assault. This, and the subsequent phases of consolidation and exploitation, are critical in determining whether the amphibious landing will be able to establish a sufficiently extended beachhead to ensure continuous troop landing and to provide the space to manoeuvre for subsequent operations.

OPPOSED AND UNOPPOSED LANDINGS

Securing the beach is possibly the most complex and dangerous part of an amphibious operation: it requires the careful coordination and control of many different parts of the force by the amphibious commander. Even when there is no opposition, landing a force can be difficult. For example, at Guadalcanal on 7 August 1942, scheduling and logistic problems quickly introduced chaos into the landing operation, despite the absence of a Japanese beach defence. If

LEFT: Marines wade ashore during the invasion of Tarawa. Landing boats and barges brought them to within 500yds (457m) of the beach, but the coraled bottom prevented the boats from coming closer to the shore. The potential vulnerability of the troops to enemy fire is evident.

ABOVE: Palau Island, under US air attack on 30 March 1944. Against small islands such as these, achieving an unopposed landing is almost impossible if the defenders are deployed in any strength.

BELOW: The assault against Iwo Jima, 19 February 1944. Mount Suribachi is in the background. The mountain had been heavily fortified by the Japanese. This photo readily conveys the exposed position of the attacking forces during the assault phase.

the process of sending the landing force ashore is opposed by an enemy force defending the landing site, these difficulties are multiplied many times, therefore an unopposed landing is usually preferable. By using deception, surprise, preparatory gunfire, unexpected routes, night attack and so on, the amphibious commander hopes to land his force before the enemy can move to oppose it, or at least to reduce opposition to the minimum possible. For states with limited amphibious capabilities – which include most states in the contemporary world – opposed landings against well-defended beaches may constitute an operation of last resort. Instead, the amphibious

commander may well choose to balance the military utility of a landing beach against ease of landing; in the Falklands war, for example, the choice of San Carlos was made because of the greater likelihood of achieving an unopposed landing compared with going ashore at the prime objective, the island's capital, Port Stanley. While an unopposed landing was conducted, once ashore the force was then faced with a 60-mile (96km) advance over inhospitable terrain in order to reach the capital.

Although an unopposed landing is clearly preferable for an amphibious commander, it may not be an option. It may be that the objective area is simply too small to contain a landing site that will avoid enemy defences, as was the case with many of the Pacific islands which were defended by the Japanese in World War II. Alternatively, the number of possible landing sites may be relatively small, or the enemy may have sufficient forces to defend all of the useful approaches, as was the case at Normandy. Sometimes, an unopposed beach is too far from centres of operational importance to be relevant. Even if an unopposed landing is hoped for, a prudent commander will make contingencies in case enemy forces are present at the time of the landing.

THE LANDING PHASE

The capture of the beach is the task of the landing force, which is carried aboard the amphibious task force. The exact process of getting the landing force ashore and then securing the beach varies with each situation. The amphibious commander's plan will have to take into account local conditions, such as the nature of the opposition, the capabilities of his own force and the geography of the objective area. Whatever the plan, the main imperative is usually the same in every case: to ensure a rapid build-up of combat power on the landing site which is great enough to defeat enemy counter-attacks and to ensure the integrity of the beachhead. Whatever the details of specific plans, operations to secure the beach often pass through several stages.

THE ORGANIZATION OF FORCES

The first of these stages is the effective organization of forces. As far as possible,

the assault needs a force that is immediately ready for combat. The assaulting force will be landed in waves, with the sequence of the waves corresponding to the tasks that they will have to perform. The transfer of elements from some ships to others – commonly known as 'cross-decking' – may be necessary here. The amphibious force will be reorganized once it is in the objective area in order to ensure an effective offload of the landing force. The ships which are not immediately needed for the assault will be deployed on the outer rim of the objective area, in waters cleared of mines and protected by escorts. Closer in, a transport area will be established; this is where the troop transports are deployed. Near this, an area called the 'assembly area' may be designated; this is where the assault waves assemble prior to the attack. Whatever the terminology used, there will often be a 'line of departure', which is parallel to the beach; from this line of departure, final movement to the beach is conducted. Boat lanes, which are designated routes cleared of obstacles, will extend from this line to the beach. To seaward of the line of departure, 'approach lanes' extend into the 'transport area'. Other sea areas may be established either for the deployment of NGS ships or for 'floating dumps' which serve to provide immediate logistic support of the assault.

THE OBJECTIVE AREA

The next stage of the operation to secure the beachhead is called the 'preparation of the objective area'. During this phase, air defence over the amphibious objective area will be enhanced to protect the vulnerable amphibious task group. Airstrikes and NGS will be conducted against enemy defensive positions in and around the beaches and landing zones. Supporting fire will be intensified immediately before the assault-waves are launched in order to neutralize the enemy forces – particularly the artillery or missile positions – that might interfere with the final approach and deployment of the landing force. Ideally, this supporting fire continues until the landing force is very close to the enemy, suppressing the defences for as long as possible; it then switches to the flanks of the beach or to a point just inland to

interdict enemy reinforcements or disrupt counter-attacks. Mine counter-measure efforts and operations to clear beach defences may proceed in parallel. However, effective fire support is often difficult to achieve. Good intelligence, reconnaissance and command and control facilities are required if preparatory activities are to be properly coordinated with the assault. Often, even rudimentary enemy defences are able to survive massive pre-bombardment. Sometimes, problems in synchronizing supporting fire may result in mistaken attacks upon one's own troops, as happened in the assault on Tanambogo during the Guadalcanal campaign when US troops were struck down by their own fire support.

SHIP-TO-SHORE MOVEMENT

The subsequent stage of the operation is known as 'ship-to-shore movement'. If the transport group consists of specialist amphibious shipping, then they may project the landing forces directly onto the beach or, if 'vertical envelopment' is being conducted, onto helicopter landing zones. Otherwise, the forces may be disembarked from the transport group into helicopters, landing craft, amphibious vehicles or boats. Generally, once launched, the seaborne forces will move to a designated assembly area where they will form into assault-waves before, at a pre-arranged time, they begin the dangerous approach to the shore. Ship-to-shore movement may be closely accompanied by airborne landings, as was the case during Operation Overlord. Naturally, the landing force is exceedingly

BELOW: Royal Marines prepare to demolish obstacles on the Normandy beaches. Often these defences had been booby-trapped with explosives and mines.

ABOVE: Marine raiders pull away from the side of a fast transport in rubber boats during 1942. Disembarking troops is a complex and often dangerous process. Ideally, the troops involved should undergo training in the necessary procedures to ensure that transfer to the assault craft is conducted in a quick and orderly fashion.

vulnerable during the transition ashore, and it is vital that the movements of the various waves are properly coordinated with fire support operations. Protection during movement to the beach can be provided through 'active' measures, such as air support or anti-submarine operations, or through 'passive' measures, such as proper separation between assault elements and rapidity of movement. In recent years, alternative movement concepts have emerged, these being notably 'ship to objective manoeuvre' and 'over the horizon operations': these alternative concepts will be discussed in more depth in Chapter Nine.

The next phase of the landing operation is gaining a lodgement. Once at the shore – or the landing zones – the assault shipping and helicopters unload troops, vehicles and supplies. Here speed is vital, since the landing forces are in competition with the defenders; if, through reinforcement and counter-attack, the defence is able to build up more combat power than the landing force, then the amphibious assault may be doomed. In order to help the build-up of combat power, the initial waves of troops need to seize a bridgehead which is large enough to allow the deployment of supporting waves of troops and supplies. This is often termed 'tactical logistical space'. 'Vertical envelopment' operations by helicopters or airborne troops can help to achieve this. As the landings proceed, other operations are ongoing; tactical reconnaissance by aircraft, electronic warfare, NGS and airstrikes help to

support the assaulting force and to inflict attrition on the enemy. One dilemma for the commander is how to achieve the appropriate balance between speed and organization: a rapid offload that leads to confusion and disorganization on the beach may in fact be counter-productive.

Once the assaulting forces are ashore, operations inland can commence. These operations try to bring together the disparate seaborne, heliborne, airborne and air-landed elements of the attack. As operations ashore continue, the commander of the landing force will need to continually review the progress of the offensive, putting in requests for support as and when needed. The landing force commander needs to balance the scope of inland operations against the danger of prematurely exhausting and weakening the forces.

After the planned initial assault waves have been sent, supporting ship–to–shore movement will be required. This may be the deployment of reserves, perhaps at the request of the landing force commander. However, if the assaulting force is to win the race to build up superior combat power, and if a viable beachhead is to be established then the amphibious force commander will need to start a 'heavy offload' of supplies, combat support units such as artillery and combat service support personnel as soon as is practicable. If the landing goes well, then the burden of support and command of the assault should shift relatively quickly from the forces afloat to the beachhead.

Depending upon the circumstances, provision will need to be made early on for the movement of forces from the beachhead and back onto transports, a process which is called 'shore-to-ship' movement. This may be necessary because the amphibious assault has failed and a general withdrawal is required. Shore-to-ship movement may also be ordered because a portion of the initial landing force is required elsewhere, or because casualties or prisoners-of-war need to be evacuated.

BATTLE MANAGEMENT
Speed and flexibility are important in securing the beach, but achieving speed and flexibility is not easy. Amphibious operations can pose enormous problems in battle management. In part, this is

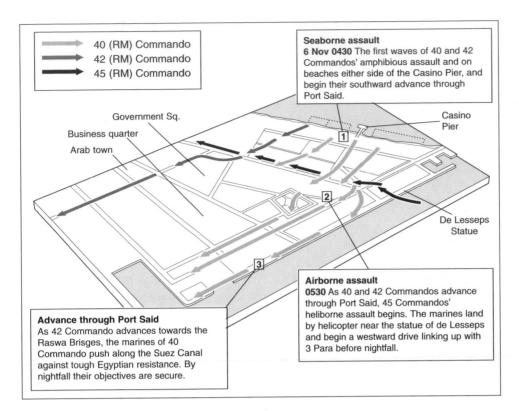

Seaborne assault
6 Nov 0430 The first waves of 40 and 42 Commandos' amphibious assault and on beaches either side of the Casino Pier, and begin their southward advance through Port Said.

40 (RM) Commando
42 (RM) Commando
45 (RM) Commando

Government Sq.
Business quarter
Arab town

Casino Pier

De Lesseps Statue

Advance through Port Said
As 42 Commando advances towards the Raswa Brisges, the marines of 40 Commando push along the Suez Canal against tough Egyptian resistance. By nightfall their objectives are secure.

Airborne assault
0530 As 40 and 42 Commandos advance through Port Said, 45 Commandos' heliborne assault begins. The marines land by helicopter near the statue of de Lesseps and begin a westward drive linking up with 3 Para before nightfall.

LEFT: The Suez landing, 1956. This beach assault was accompanied by vertical envelopment operations by helicopter-borne troops, the first of their kind.

because they are joint operations and require the coordination of many different components: the landing force; the maritime component; fire support elements; airborne and air-landed troops; land-based air; special forces and so on. Well-developed command and control facilities and secure communications are important in managing the amphibious battle, yet they are also beyond the means of many countries. Communications problems can be multiplied by a lack of interoperability between services or, in coalition operations, between different countries, as was the case between British and French contingents at Suez in 1956. One decision the landing force commander will have to take is when to transfer his headquarters ashore. Organizational efforts can help to make the beach landing easier: detailed planning, timetables, rehearsals and drills can all improve coordination of the operation itself. Although this will improve the operation's speed, however, it may undermine its flexibility if any special local circumstances require a change in approach.

CASE STUDY: GALLIPOLI, APRIL 1915

The main landings at Gallipoli began on 25 April 1915. The wider objectives of the attack were to take the Gallipoli peninsula, allowing a naval force to transit the Dardanelles to Constantinople where operations were designed to bring down the Turkish Government. Few thought that the operation would be an easy one, and the commander Sir Ian Hamilton was under no illusions as to the scale of his task. The Gallipoli peninsula was high and rocky, offering good defensive terrain. There were only four practicable landing sites, all of which were dominated by high ground. Operational surprise had already been lost, thanks to

BELOW: ANZAC troops sail towards the Gallipoli peninsula in April 1915. The April landings were hampered at all levels by a lack of specialist transport and assault vessels.

earlier naval operations and poor security, and the Turkish defenders had been reinforced and had dug in. Their German commander, Liman Von Sanders, adopted a deep defence, keeping a portion of his troops in reserve for a counter-attack. In addition, the early part of the operation was dogged by organizational problems: there was a lack of specialist shipping; the transports had not been 'tactically loaded' prior to their arrival in-theatre (the force therefore had to be sent to Egypt to re-organize); and Lemnos, the island chosen as the main base of the operation, was lacking in facilities.

Nevertheless, by 25 April the invasion force had assembled off the coast of Gallipoli. Here the amphibious force was helped by the lack of Turkish sea-denial efforts: no mines had been sown and no attempt was made by Turkish naval forces to sortie out and, furthermore, German U-boat assistance did not arrive until May. Hamilton planned to try to gain local superiority in numbers by using deception and surprise. One assault would be launched against the tip of the

Gallipoli peninsula at Cape Helles. Here 17,000 men would land on five beaches, designated 'X', 'Y', 'W', 'V' and 'S'. Another major landing, this time of the Australia and New Zealand Army Corps (ANZAC), which was 30,000 strong, was to be made further up the coast at Gabba Tepe, starting at 0430 hours. Diversionary operations were launched to the north at Bulair by the Royal Naval Division, and to the south on the Asiatic side of the Dardanelles by a French division. The ANZAC assault would be launched in darkness and the Helles attacks would be launched in the early morning light after NGS preparation from accompanying battleships. The objective was to land the force and seize a bridgehead that included the vital high ground to the east of the landing sites.

There were extensive difficulties during the landing. Attacking in darkness gained the advantage of surprise and provided protection from defensive fire, but it also made navigation difficult. The ANZAC troops mistakenly landed at Ari Burnu – over 1 mile (1.6km) north of the intended landing site – and were halted by the terrain and Turkish counter-attacks. They managed to maintain a slender bridgehead there, but only just. At Helles, portions of the attack were very successful and managed to land virtually unopposed. The 2000 troops at 'Y' beach faced no opposition at all, and were soon able to reach their objective. Here they remained, however, receiving neither reinforcements nor new orders, until eventually Turkish reinforcements drove them back. On other beaches, the Turkish opposition was able to inflict appalling casualties. An old steamer, the *River Clyde*, had been modified as a primitive landing ship with doors cut into its side and machine-guns placed on its bows. This was run ashore at 'V' beach with the intention that its troops quickly disembark. However, the Turkish defenders had survived the pre-bombardment, and they slaughtered the attackers as they tried to exit the steamer, turning the water around it red with blood. A reprieve was only provided by night, which allowed more forces to be brought ashore. Attempts to push forward and seize the high ground in further attacks failed, with the Turks bringing up reserves. Turkish hopes of driving the

BELOW: Under Turkish shell fire, British troops unload stores at Sedd-ul-Bahr. Having failed to take the high ground in April 1915, British and ANZAC troops and their supplies were crammed into shallow bridgeheads well within range of Turkish guns.

LEFT: HMS *Cornwallis* firing salvoes at Turkish fortifications. Spotting, coordinating and controlling NGS proved difficult. In May 1915 the arrival of German U-boats forced the withdrawal of all but one of the battleships.

Allied troops from the beach were dashed through a combination of the excellent defensive terrain and useful NGS support. By the beginning of May, the landing force was established ashore but it was well short of the initial objectives.

A number of factors impeded the success of the landing. One was the size of the Allied force which, given the level of attrition, was too small to sustain offensive operations for very long. Another was the disappointing performance of NGS: it was initially effective at suppressing the defence, but the difficulty in spotting for it and the cover provided by terrain made it less useful for destruction or for interdicting the movement of Turkish reserves, which often advanced at night. Another challenge was the lack of appropriate equipment, including dedicated landing craft capable of moving large numbers of troops quickly, and organic fire support, such as mortars and artillery, to use against local targets. Command and control, which quickly broke down in the confusion of the battle, proved another Achilles' heel. Despite remaining at sea during the operation – a reasonable enough decision that gave Hamilton

mobility – opportunities to commit reserves and exploit potential successes were missed. Moreover, the ship upon which Hamilton was based did not have the facilities to accommodate his military staff, and therefore they had to be spread out over several vessels; this further eroded the Allies' ability to plan and control operations.

At Gallipoli, then, the amphibious force got ashore. However, it had not been the Turkish intention to defeat the invasion at the beach, but instead to crush it with counter-attacks. In the event, both sides fell short of their objectives because neither could generate sufficient combat power to defeat the other.

CASE STUDY: DIEPPE, 1942

Dieppe provides an example of a different type of operation: the amphibious raid. The raid, launched on 19 August 1942, was the first strongly opposed landing attempted by British and Commonwealth forces since Gallipoli. Dieppe was a testing ground for doctrine, equipment and tactics concerned with the conduct of such operations. It also had a wider role – that of informing planning for later, larger landings.

The landing force involved more than 6000 troops, the bulk of whom were Canadian. Dieppe was chosen as a target because its defences were assessed as not too strong and because it was within range of Allied land-based aircraft. The plan adopted was essentially a frontal attack, supported by the landing of 60 Churchill heavy tanks. A wide assault to the flanks was rejected because it would take too long to reach Dieppe, allowing German reinforcements to move up. Early plans for an associated airborne landing were cancelled because they relied too heavily on good weather. The landings consisted of five attacks: a main landing against Dieppe beach; two flank landings launched to seal off Dieppe; and one assault on each of the extreme flanks by commandos against German coastal defence batteries. Despite high hopes of the amount of destruction and dislocation that could be inflicted on the garrison at Dieppe, the landing was a tragic failure. After 12 hours of fighting, around 60 per cent of the landing force were killed, captured or wounded.

Establishing a beachhead at Dieppe proved to be problematic. The geography of the beaches was one factor: the high cliffs overlooking them provided good defensive positions. Another difficulty was that the German defences turned out to be much better developed than had been anticipated. These problems were worsened when the critical element of surprise was lost during the landing. The initial plan for heavy bombing of Dieppe the night before had been cancelled because it was felt that there was more advantage to be had by maintaining surprise. However, as eight destroyers, seven LSI (Landing Ship Infantry), 24 LCT (Landing Craft Tank) and another 100 minor craft approached the coast, they made contact with some German transports and this led to a German coast alert at 0458 hours. The sequencing of the attack waves also contributed to the defeat. The commando landings were launched at 0450 hours but the main landings were not due to start until 0520 hours, and this half-hour period was long enough for the Dieppe garrison to be alerted. In any case, the eastern flank mission arrived on the beach 15 minutes late, by which time the garrison had been alerted. The main attack left on time, but the LCTs arrived 10 or 15 minutes late. This left the infantry on the beach at the

BELOW: Canadian troops approach the beach at Dieppe. Smoke quickly obscured the beaches making it difficult for the landing force and the commander, Major General Roberts, to see how the operation was unfolding.

LEFT: Canadian tanks litter the beaches at Dieppe. Only 27 of the 60-strong tank force were landed. Of these, none could penetrate into Dieppe itself because of German anti-tank obstacles.

BELOW: The bloody repulse at Dieppe on 19 August 1942 convinced the Allies that any future large amphibious assault into Europe should initially avoid major ports. It also convinced Hitler that it was possible to defeat an invasion at the water's edge. Both conclusions influenced strategy for the later Normandy invasions.

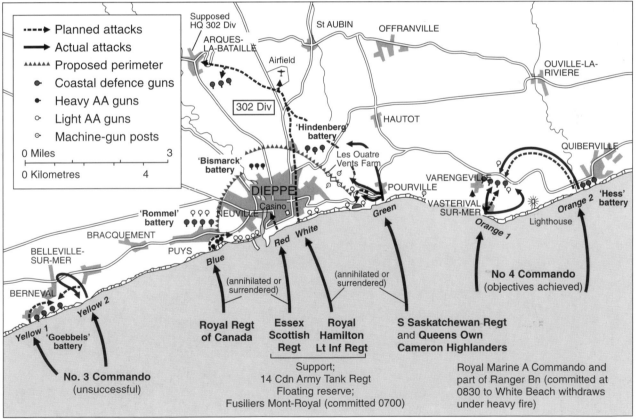

critical early phase without tank support. The effect of supporting fire was also disappointing for the Allies; there was little in the way of deep operations, so German reinforcements were able to move up rapidly. Although the eight destroyers and fighter cover suppressed the German defences until the landing craft of the main force reached the beach, they inflicted little actual damage; once the bombardment lifted, the defences were able to pour a withering fire on the attacking force. Furthermore, the landing force commander was afloat, without a

ABOVE: The beach full of Canadian casualties and equipment at Dieppe. Inadequate fire support failed to suppress the enemy defences and the assault was launched into the teeth of withering defensive fire. The Canadians suffered 68 per cent casualties.

clear picture of what was going on, and consequently mistakenly committed his reserves to one of the failed landings instead of reinforcing success.

Although the Dieppe operation validated the importance of some assault concepts – such as the utility of specialized amphibious equipment in facilitating ship-to-shore movement – it also seemed to reinforce the lesson learnt from Gallipoli that opposed landings were dangerous enterprises. Dieppe

illustrated that, if the momentum of the initial attack was lost, the assault was in trouble. This momentum could be facilitated by surprise or by heavy fire support. Once surprise had failed at Dieppe, there was insufficient supporting fire – from aircraft, NGS or tanks – either to restore forward movement or to impede the build-up of enemy troops. The tempo of the operation was quickly lost as the troops became pinned down on the beach. Without a clear idea of how the operation was unfolding, there was little scope for the commanding officer to restore the situation.

CASE STUDY: IWO JIMA, 1945

In contrast to Gallipoli and Dieppe, the US assault against Iwo Jima on 19 February 1945 illustrates that opposed landings can be successfully conducted even where the defence is extremely strong. Iwo Jima was regarded as a potentially vital airbase in the war against Japan. The Japanese defenders were well aware of the imminence of the attack, and this was furthered by US pre-landing operations in the months and days before the actual invasion. The volcanic island offered excellent defensive terrain, with the dominating feature, Mount Suribachi, providing a good observation and gun position. The Japanese garrison of around 21,000 men was supported by over 400

RIGHT: Iwo Jima was the largest Marine assault of World War II. Despite the enormous preparatory fire, many of the Japanese defences survived, forcing the three assaulting Marine divisions into a grim attritional struggle.

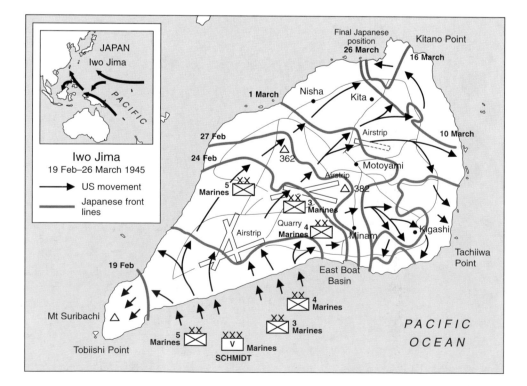

artillery pieces, mortars and rockets and a Tank Regiment. It had managed to make good use of the available terrain, and had constructed an intricate network of more than 600 gun positions and 17 miles (27km) of tunnels.

Despite the formidable defences, and notwithstanding the savage fighting that took place, the US landing on Iwo Jima was extremely successful. On D-Day, 450 vessels of the US Fifth Fleet assembled offshore. Aboard these 450 vessels were the assault force, 4th and 5th Marine Division, with 3rd Marine Division provided as a floating reserve. A heavy pre-bombardment began at 0640 hours, then from 0805 hours to 0825 hours close support ships moved into position 1000yds (914m) offshore and aircraft launched a final strike against the defenders. The first wave started the 4000yd (3656m), 45-minute journey to shore, and landed on the beach at 0902 hours. They met only light resistance and additional forces rapidly followed. At 0945 hours, very heavy Japanese counter-fire began, and the Marines were initially pinned down 200–300yds (182–274m) in from the shore. However, by 1030 hours, elements of all the assault battalions were ashore, and tanks, bulldozers and artillery also began to arrive.

The speed of the build-up allowed the Marines to push inland and, by nightfall of 19 February, they were able to secure the neck of land cutting off Mount Suribachi. Despite having taken 2500 casualties, the assault had successfully put ashore 30,000 men on the first day. Taking the island would require more than 30 days of difficult fighting, but it

was clear by the end of 19 February that the amphibious element of the assault had been a success.

The American success in securing the beach at Iwo Jima reflected a number of factors. The weight and longevity of preparatory operations was one consideration. There was a massive 74-day air bombardment and the Navy also provided a creeping barrage for the assaulting troops; this was the first time it had been used in the Pacific. Also important were the amphibious capabilities which had been developed by the USA by 1945. These included tank landing craft, Landing Ship, Mediums

ABOVE: Iwo Jima from the air, February 1945, showing Mount Suribachi, and the beaches. The US success was facilitated by its almost complete air superiority.

BELOW: Troops of the Fourth Marine Division storm ashore against Iwo Jima. The lack of initial resistance reflected the Japanese belief that a forward defence of the beach would not be able to survive in the face of US pre-landing attacks.

ABOVE: The Atlantic Wall. Crewmen of a 3.9in (100mm) M38 (t) Czech-made howitzer camouflage their position. The bulk of the German gun positions were still operational when the US troops landed despite earlier air and NGS attacks.

(LSMs) and Landing Craft, Vehicle and Personnels (LCVPs) and a specialist amphibious vehicle, the Landing Vehicle, Tracked (LVT) capable of carrying troops not just to the beach but across it as well. As many as 482 LVTs carried the initial assault battalions into action. The first wave was escorted by LVTs armed with 3in (75mm) howitzers, giving the initial landing force organic heavy support. The number of specialist vehicles available meant that two divisions could be used in the immediate assault, and follow-on forces such as tanks and heavy equipment could be brought ashore quickly. Success must also be attributed to the effective command and control of the operation. In addition to having a dedicated amphibious command ship, USS *Eldorado*, the US commander led a relatively experienced force. Many had been through the campaigns in the Gilbert Islands, Marshalls and Marianas. This experience, along with their extensive preparations – including practice landings over mock-ups of the

Iwo Jima defences – helped to ensure that the landings were largely executed according to plan.

These advantages put the Japanese defenders on the horns of a dilemma. Earlier defensive experiences seemed to show the Japanese that defences based along the beach line could not survive US preparatory fire. On Iwo Jima, the defence concept was based more upon an inland deployment, which would counter-attack the US forces once they had landed; this was one of the reasons why the main force of Japanese fire arrived after the Marines had hit the beach. Yet, as Iwo Jima proved, a more mobile defence in depth was equally problematic; the USA had the equipment, personnel, and experience to land large numbers of troops and heavy equipment very quickly, and this allowed them to build a critical mass of combat power before an effective counter-attack could be mounted. Moreover, the USA's overwhelming air and NGS support could slow and fragment the counter-attacks as they emerged. The lesson was that a large, experienced and well-supported force could succeed in securing the beach even against formidable defences.

CASE STUDY: OMAHA BEACH

The landing by the US 5th Corps involved some of the most difficult fighting of the Normandy assault. The landing force, Force O, consisted of 34,000 men and 3300 vehicles. The attacking force had two advantages: heavy preparatory fire support from bombers and ships, and good intelligence on the nature of the defences. Recognizing the need for heavy organic support, command sent in tanks and artillery in landing craft and amphibious vehicles with the early waves. A total of 96 tanks were converted into Duplex Drive (DD) vehicles, giving them an amphibious capability. The attacking force was also well provided with specialist amphibious transport.

Despite these advantages, the attack was not likely to be easy; the defences on Omaha were formidable. The beach was enclosed by rocky bluffs, providing positions from which an enfilade fire could – and was – brought to bear on the attackers. The beach was mined and the defending force, the experienced 352nd Infantry Regiment, was protected by entrenchments, pillboxes and emplacements. The defences were arrayed in some depth, with additional mines, trenches and machine-gun positions behind the forward line. However, as the landing operation unfolded, severe problems developed. Ship-to-shore movement proved to be chaotic. The weather was atrocious, with poor visibility and heavy seas. Many of the assaulting troops spent four hours or so getting to the beach in transports and several of the smaller craft foundered. Most of the DD tanks in the first wave were launched 6000yds (5486m) off-shore, and many of them sank in the

BELOW: US troops leave DUKWs and other landing craft on Omaha beach, 7 June 1944. The success of the Normandy landings as a whole was supported by two years of Allied experience in other amphibious operations that led to the development of new doctrine, training and equipment.

heavy swell. Much of the supporting artillery was lost. For example, the 111th Field Artillery Battalion saved only one of its 4.1in (105mm) howitzers. Engineer teams also suffered heavy losses in men and equipment. Supporting NGS suppressed the German defences in the transit to the shore; however, the barrage lifted when the first wave was 800yds (732m) from the beach and a telling German fire commenced. Moreover, as the landing craft approached the beach, sandbanks and extensive underwater beach obstacles halted the first wave short of the shoreline, forcing them to disembark into the sea. Despite this, within about 30 minutes, 1000 troops were on the beach. However, they were confused, disorganized and in no position to press the attack against the defenders. The 10-mile (16km) stretch of beach became for a time a killing ground, and the US Fifth Corps sustained 2000 casualties. Some tanks did manage to get ashore, but many parts of the assault-wave had no armoured support at all. Logistic operations proved almost impossible under the enemy fire and less than 5 per cent of essential supplies got ashore on the first day. Thus, although the troops had succeeded in

reaching the beach, they lacked the strength and cohesion to fight their way inland and the force was exceedingly vulnerable to German counter-attack. Nevertheless, the beach was gradually secured. Despite heavy casualties, engineers began clearing paths through the beach defences and LCTs brought in tanks of the 743rd Tank battalion. Gradually, the assault force infiltrated forward and by nightfall had achieved a secure beachhead, even if it was much less extensive than planned.

Critical to the landing's eventual success was that 5th Corps was able to continue to send waves of reinforcements ashore, whereas the Germans were not reinforced. Over time, the balance of combat power tipped in favour of the USA and some forward movement was restored. In part, this situation was due to Allied command of the sea and to air superiority; this ensured the protection of the large numbers of reserve troops and allowed the US forces to inflict attrition on the defence, even when the landing force was weakly positioned. 'Deep attacks' from NGS and especially air power helped to seal off the battlefield, and impeded the movement of enemy reserves. A critical contributor

BELOW: US soldiers under heavy artillery and machine-gun fire at Normandy. Some hide behind the beach obstacles, others follow a tank out of the water. The chaos and confusion that can quickly engulf an opposed landing is readily apparent.

to success, however, was the way in which the Allies succeeded in creating confusion and dislocation in the German High Command. Prior to the landing, Field Marshal Rommel made repeated efforts to move 12th SS Panzer Divison and Panzer Lehr to a position between St Lo and Carentan. If they had been there, the Omaha landing would have been smashed. The decision to release reserves was not taken until late afternoon on D–Day, however. Surprise, an inability to engage in air reconnaissance thanks to Allied air superiority, the blocking of radar, the bombing of transport nodes, and prior Allied deception made it difficult for the Germans to tell if the Normandy landing was merely a diversion for a main landing at the Pas de Calais. In this critical period of indecision, a decisive mass of force was building on Omaha beach that would finally overcome the defence and allow a secure beachhead to be established.

CONCLUSION

Securing the beach is a complex and dangerous operation, and this was a lesson which was demonstrated by the outcomes at Gallipoli and Dieppe. When the operation does go wrong, the results can be disastrous. Ideally, the assaulting force will attempt to use a variety of techniques to secure an unopposed landing. However, in some circumstances, unopposed landings are not practical or achievable. Yet, as Omaha and Iwo Jima demonstrate, the amphibious assault can be conducted against a strongly defended beach.

The history of opposed operations shows that a number of factors are important in achieving a successful operation: good preparation; sound planning; sufficient forces; proper equipment; local sea and air superiority; and effective command, control and communications. These elements can allow the attacker to win the crucial fight on the beach, building up his combat power in the objective area at a faster rate than the defender, and so creating a viable bridgehead into which reinforcements can be deployed. Once this bridgehead is attained, then the landing forces can begin to reorganize themselves in preparation for a breakout in order to exploit their success.

ABOVE: A Centurion tank is landed during the Suez crisis in 1956. Four Landing Craft Tanks (LCTs) landed 14 waterproof tanks from C Squadron, 6 Royal Tank Regiment. 40 and 42 Commando landed at 0450. The first tanks arrived 10 minutes later.

CHAPTER FIVE

CONSOLIDATION AND EXPLOITATION

The development of the initial lodgement can decide whether a successful landing translates into a successful campaign.

Amphibious landings are a means; they are not an end. Landing a force ashore can be a complex and dangerous task in itself but it would be wrong to equate a successful amphibious landing with a successful amphibious operation. The success of an operation needs to be judged in terms of what is achieved after the landing. Successful amphibious operations will usually require both the consolidation of the initial lodgement and also, following that, a period of exploitation. During this period of exploitation, land and air forces move inland in order to capitalize on the initial advantages – such as surprise – which have resulted from the landing itself. Of course, the ambition and scope of each amphibious operations varies and this will dictate how much consolidation and exploitation is required. For example, the objectives of Soviet desant operations were usually tactical in nature, whereas the Inchon landings aimed to have a operational effect. The relevance of consolidation and exploitation will vary also according to the type of operation to be conducted: they will be of little

LEFT: 5th Marine Division, Iwo Jima, 28 February 1945. A beach on the northern end of the island receives rations, water and ammunition. An amphibious landing must consolidate a sufficiently large beachhead to allow the necessary logistics support to be organized and built up for the subsequent phases of the operation.

ABOVE: US LSTs unload trucks on the island of Nisida near Naples in World War II. Exploitation will often depend upon having sufficient transport to move supplies from the beachhead to fighting units further inland. Unless this can be done, the advancing forces will rapidly outdistance their logistic support and the attack will grind to a halt.

or no importance for withdrawals; in demonstrations, their significance will depend upon whether a landing is to be carried out and the size of diversion required; for amphibious raids, the relevance of consolidating and exploiting the landing will depend upon how ambitious the objectives are. For most theatre-entry scenarios, consolidation and exploitation of the landing is vital if the amphibious assault is to have operational and strategic effect.

CONSOLIDATION

The first objective of consolidation is to reinforce the integrity of the lodgement area. The second objective is to prepare for subsequent exploitation. Once the initial assault-waves have established a viable beachhead, a number of activities can then begin in order to facilitate the build-up of combat power.

The third important objective during consolidation is to develop the logistic infrastructure at the beachhead. Bulk combat supplies contained within STUFT and logistic landing ships will be offloaded and efforts will be made to increase the size and efficiency of logistic

throughput. This is done in various ways, perhaps by repairing or capturing enemy ports, building quays or moorings, or repairing or building air strips. In the assault on the Philippines in 1941, Japanese landings at Batan island on 9 December and against Aparri and Vigan the following day on 10 December were intended to seize airfields which could be used to ensure a quick consolidation of the attack. In order to facilitate the arrival of new forces and supplies, the lodgement area is divided up, allocating some parts of it to specific tasks or arms. Such 'real estate management' is necessary in order to avoid confusion and to ensure the most effective use of assets. These designated areas may include reserved areas for artillery, forward-operating bases for helicopters, and arming and replenishment points for the landed forces. Usually, reinforcements – or 'follow-on forces' as they are widely known – will be landed quickly, this being done perhaps from an afloat reserve. Often these include heavy equipment such as tanks and heavy artillery, and if this is the case then the beachhead needs to be large enough not only to protect the follow-on forces as they land but also to sustain them. The process of landing follow-on forces can be helped by the use of specialist equipment. During Operation Husky, the invasion of Sicily, for example, new equipment was introduced, such as Landing Ship Tanks (LSTs), large-capacity craft with flat bottoms and bow doors which allowed heavy equipment to be landed directly onto the shore. This new equipment was in part responsible for the overall success of the operation.

THE REORGANIZATION OF FORCES

Efforts to build up combat power in the lodgement area will run concurrent with the reorganization of the forces on the beach. Since subsequent operations will usually focus on land battles, then, if it is not re-embarked, the landing force will be integrated with reinforcements and prepared for a combined-arms land battle. For example, after the Inchon landings had taken place, the Marine forces who had conducted them became part of the land campaign. While the specialist Marine training and equipment such as LVTs were found to be useful, especially when used for river crossings, the Marines were nevertheless used in a conventional infantry role under command of the army. All of the forces within the lodgement area are thus tactically reorganized to ensure that the various command, logistic, intelligence, strike and combat components are prepared for a coordinated movement from that area. To help with this, command and control arrangements must change. Once the landing force commander is sure that he has a force capable of independent action ashore, he moves his headquarters from ships to a land location. He then assumes control of the land battle. However, if larger land formations arrive, the landing force commander may well be made subordinate to these formations.

BUILD-UP TO THE BREAKOUT

Consolidation will also depend upon continued military operations. These are usually both defensive, in terms of defending the landing force's ability to build up combat power, and offensive, involving attacks on the enemy's ability both to reinforce and to counter-attack.

Defensive operations may involve combat air patrols above the objective area, anti-submarine patrols, NGS, defence of sea lines of communications (SLOCs) and so on. Offensive operations may involve air or NGS interdiction of enemy troop formations, and the destruction of transport and supply nodes. Sea control will remain a key objective; if the enemy is able to seriously hamper the flow of friendly supplies and reinforcements through naval or air attacks on shipping or disembarkation points, then it may be able to prevent effective consolidation of the landing in the medium to long term, even if the landing has been successful in the short term. Conversely, if the enemy relies on its sea reinforcements, as Japanese garrisons often did in the Pacific, sea control may help constrain the enemy build-up. Land operations inland may also be required for one of several reasons: to link up smaller beachheads if multiple landings have been used; to expand the lodgement area for receiving additional forces and supplies; or to capture the logistic facilities – such as ports – which were not taken in the initial assault. The problems caused by having too shallow a lodgement area were illustrated by Operation Avalanche, the Allied landings at Salerno on 9 September 1943. Here, the landing force was successfully deployed ashore but then

BELOW: A regimental command post on Iwo Jima, 8 March 1945. Although the relatively small size of the island limited the distances involved in exploitation, it also created difficulties in carving out sufficient 'tactical logistical space' within which to consolidate. This command post, between the sea and the sheer cliffs against which the Japanese were backed up, was almost in the front lines.

was unable to secure more than a shallow bridgehead in the week after that. This allowed German fire to be brought onto the Allied ports of Salerno and Vietri and onto Montecorvino airfield, which was to seriously impede the Allied build-up. As a result, the Germans were able to reinforce faster than the Allies could and therefore commenced major counter-attacks, beginning on 12 September, which made an Allied evacuation a possibility. Heavy air support and NGS eventually turned the situation around, but, even so, the Allies did not really manage to consolidate their position until as late as mid-October.

EXPLOITATION

With consolidation complete, the forces in the beachhead then attempt to achieve a breakout. At this point in the proceedings, the operation will take on the characteristics of a land campaign.

The challenges posed by exploitation depend on the operational context, which is shaped by factors such as the overall objectives; the combat power of the opposition; the terrain; whether air superiority has been achieved; the logistic situation and so on. Limited objectives will undoubtedly make exploitation easier. In the US and British Torch

landings of 8 November 1942 in North Africa, extensive exploitation ultimately was not required. Once the US and British forces were able to demonstrate to the French that the initial landings had been consolidated, the Vichy government in North Africa asked for terms and an armistice was arranged by noon on 10 November. Clear objectives also help the process of exploitation – knowing what is to be achieved allows early planning for the breakout – but clear objectives are not always attainable. This was the case during the Falklands conflict when the landing force was ordered to consolidate at San Carlos pending the arrival of reinforcements, even though it was left without a clear idea of its role in any subsequent land campaign. Exploitation is clearly more difficult when conducted against a strong and skilful enemy; for this reason, surprise, air superiority and NGS are important for success. Sometimes, however, it is not the strength of the enemy that causes problems, but his mode of fighting. For example, many amphibious landings were conducted in the Vietnam war. These mainly centred around search-and-destroy missions, such as those of the 'Deckhouse' series, which involved combined helicopter and seaborne assault missions. However,

BELOW: US Marines on New Georgia Island, New Guinea, August 1943. The thick jungle made exploitation inland very difficult. Because of this, General MacArthur instead used many sequential amphibious landings along the coast during this particular campaign.

LEFT: British Royal Marines of 45 Commando ride a BV202 in the Falklands. The BV is an all-terrain vehicle, and it proved an essential supplement to the available British transport in the harsh Falklands terrain. Nevertheless, as the line of troops behind shows, British exploitation depended primarily on the stamina of soldiers marching on foot.

exploitation of the landings brought with it all the problems associated with counter-insurgency operations, notably the difficulty in finding and pinning the enemy. Bad terrain can favour consolidation by inhibiting the movement of enemy forces to the landing zone, but it can also create difficulties in pushing forward, as was the case in the Falklands. Rapid exploitation usually requires a sufficient number of exit points leading from the beach in order to allow the land force to move quickly and utilize all of its available combat power. Exploitation will have to be sustained by adequate supplies and material, and not only will these have to be landed at the beach or airfield, but they will then also have to be moved forward over logistic lines which, if exploitation is occurring, will lengthen over time.

A dilemma is associated with the exploitation phase, and this is how to strike the balance between consolidation and exploitation. Although the consolidation period of an operation is designed to create the conditions for successful exploitation, it is difficult to determine how much consolidation will be needed for success. On the one hand, there are a range of difficulties associated with premature exploitation: lengthening logistic lines; out-distancing fire support;

lengthening communications lines; and the possibility of succumbing to a rapid enemy counter-attack, or at least of reaching a 'culminating point' too early, where the attack becomes too weak to push on before the objectives have been taken. On the other hand, spending too long on consolidating the landing position may also be counter-productive, and might throw away the important element of surprise, thus yielding the initiative to the enemy. Periods spent consolidating may give the enemy time to recover its equilibrium, and to consolidate its own position, which then makes exploitation even more problematic. This dilemma has been heightened in the modern age because in mechanized warfare defenders using internal lines can often rush heavy forces to a landing area much faster than the amphibious force can.

CASE STUDY: GUADALCANAL, 1942

US operations at Guadalcanal demonstrate some of the difficulties that can plague consolidation of an amphibious landing. Codenamed Operation Watchtower, the occupation of Guadalcanal was undertaken to protect Australia. It was also intended as an initial part of the Allied counter-offensive into the Solomon Islands. US forces landed

ABOVE: 3rd battalion, 28th US Marines engage in a frontal assault on Japanese positions on Iwo Jima. The confined island environment meant that exploitation was achieved more through attrition than manoeuvre. The battalion gained 200yds (183m) of ground in this assault at the cost of 30 lives.

unopposed on the main island of Guadalcanal on 7 August 1942. The only Japanese presence – which was a labour battalion engaged in the process of constructing an airfield – fled from the US troops and within 24 hours over 11,000 US Marines were landed on the island. However, despite this early success, US forces were not able to succeed in taking the island until February 1943.

US difficulties in consolidating and exploiting the initial landing stemmed largely from their inability to secure sea control around the island and their failure to secure air superiority over it. Control of the sea was critical because this dictated the pace at which both the USA and Japanese could reinforce their presence on the island. The Japanese had the advantage of land-based aircraft at Rabaul, which lay 600 miles (965km) north-west of Guadalcanal, and these aircraft were immediately able to disrupt US con-solidation by launching a heavy air attack against US transports which were then in the process of unloading marine equipment, artillery, food and ammunition. Fear of attack from Rabaul also led to the withdrawal of US aircraft carriers. These woes were compounded at sea on the night of 8/9 August at the

Battle of Savo Island, where a brilliant Japanese night-action left four US cruisers sunk or sinking. This, combined with the belief that Japanese carriers were near, led to the withdrawal of US transports which were carrying supplies and reinforcements to replenish the landing force.

For a period of time, therefore, the Japanese successfully achieved sea control around the island. The Japanese Navy and Airforce pounded US positions and began the movement of combat troops onto Guadalcanal in preparation for counter-attacks. Fortuitously for the US troops on the island, they could use the equipment left behind by the Japanese construction forces, and they were able to complete the airfield. On 20 August, 19 fighters and 12 dive-bombers were flown in and, once aircraft were operating from the airfield, the Japanese naval forces could only move about safely during the night. To counter this, the Japanese established the so-called 'Tokyo Express', a night-time shuttle of fast warships which brought them supplies and reinforcements. The Tokyo Express helped build up a force of 20,000 men on the island, along with tanks and heavy artillery. However, US efforts succeeded in building up their forces to a total of 23,000 men by October.

A TEMPORARY STALEMATE

Both sides, then, were operating in circumstances of contested sea control. Each side was trying to consolidate its position on the island and each side was also preparing for an opportunity to counter-attack the other. Numerous naval clashes were brought on by attempts on both sides to bring up reinforcements. The largest of these, Santa Cruz, was fought between 24 and 26 October, when US carrier forces began a wide sweep around Santa Cruz Island into the Coral Sea in order to interdict Japanese transports. However, at Santa Cruz, despite all the US attempts at interdiction, the Japanese won a Pyrrhic victory and sunk the USS *Hornet* albeit at a very heavy cost to their aircraft.

In the event, the Japanese launched their ground attack prematurely. A combination of an underestimation of the number and quality of the defenders, and the dense jungle, which exhausted the attackers and made coordination of the attack difficult, resulted in a series of costly defeats at the hands of the US Marines. Nevertheless, the US position remained precarious; despite their efforts, Japanese naval forces could still operate at night. On the night of 13/14 October, two Japanese battleships were able to conduct a 90-minute bombardment of US Marine positions. Air raids also managed to inflict much damage and, combined with further bombardments by cruisers, the US airfield was temporarily neutralized. The Japanese were able to land six transports with 3500 men during the day and US supplies were reduced to a trickle until they were able to recommence air sorties from the airfield.

Even after the Japanese had been thrown back after the critical land battle of 23 October, the USA was not in a position to begin exploitation. Battle casualties, compounded by exhaustion, disease and the dense jungle, meant that November was spent gradually extending the defence perimeter and bringing another three divisions ashore. Japanese attempts to rebuild their forces were undermined in mid-November. An attempt by Japanese naval forces to bombard and cripple the US airfield was halted by air attack, and the US aircraft then went on to attack Japanese transports which were bringing in the Japanese 28th Division. A total of 11 transports were sunk, beached or crippled, and only 2000 men, most without equipment, managed to reach Guadalcanal. Because of the scale of its losses, Japan made the decision on 31 December 1942 to withdraw. However, even at this low point in Japanese fortunes, the USA's limited sea control prevented it from significantly intervening in the withdrawal.

The USA's difficulties in consolidating and exploiting their position thus stemmed from their inability to attain complete sea control, and it created grave problems in supporting and reinforcing their troops. This allowed the Japanese to move additional forces to the island. As it turned out, control of the island's airfield

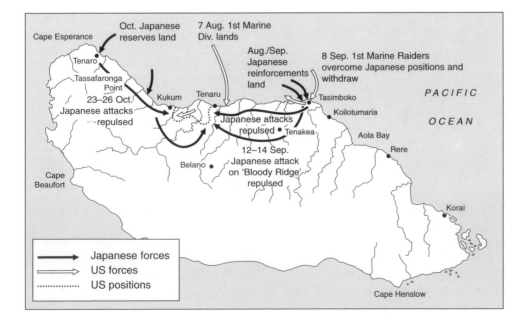

LEFT: The assault on Guadalcanal by the 1st Marine Division, between August and October 1942. Both sides found it difficult to consolidate their early positions because neither had complete sea and air superiority. In the event, the Japanese launched their attacks on the US beachhead too early, thereby effectively squandering their strength.

and the consequent ability of the USA to dominate the sea during the day all combined with Japanese errors and good defensive terrain to ensure that the USA gradually managed to build up a decisive edge in combat power.

CASE STUDY: GALLIPOLI, 1915

Earlier landings in April 1915 at Cape Helles and ANZAC Cove had succeeded in establishing a British and ANZAC force ashore. The beachhead had been consolidated and Turkish counter-attacks beaten off. However, attempts to expand the bridgehead and exploit the landings had enjoyed only limited success because of the terrain and the balance of forces. The British believed that the answer lay in another amphibious landing on the peninsula, this time further to the north at Suvla Bay. This would, it was hoped, surprise the Turks, allow a rapid movement in from the north and consequently unlock all of the positions in front of the Allied forces.

Some of the problems that had plagued the earlier landings were remedied. The terrain at Suvla was more gentle than that further to the south. The balance of forces in the Suvla area was heavily in the attacker's favour; three divisions would be available for the landing, and these would be set against a Turkish force of three battalions – or around 1500 men – which had no barbed wire or machine-guns. Instead of being landed in barges pulled by steam boats, specialist landing craft known as 'Beetles' were available. The Beetles could each carry 500 men and they had been fitted with armour and landing ramps. The fleet available to support the Suvla landings was smaller than that available for the April attack, but nevertheless it was better suited to amphibious operations. It included specialist coastal monitors for NGS, with improved anti-submarine defences, additional balloon ships to help with spotting and reconnaissance and new seaplane carriers. As many as 15 aircraft were available to help support the operation and disembarkation was to be facilitated by a mobile pier that was made of pontoons.

Exploitation was vital to the overall success of the landing; the Suvla operation had to achieve what the previous landings had not, namely the occupation of the high ground behind the immediate landing site. In this case, the high ground was a line of hills known as Ismail Oglu Tepe. Initially, the

RIGHT: At Gallipoli, the high ridges and impenetrable scrub provided favourable conditions for the defence. This allowed the British and ANZAC troops to beat off Turkish counter-attacks and consolidate their beachheads after the April 1915 landings. However, it also multiplied the difficulties of exploiting the landings in subsequent operations.

operation appeared to be running very smoothly. At around 2230 hours on 6 August, the landings began at Suvla Bay, supported by heavy assaults out of the ANZAC bridgehead at Ari Burnu. The Turks were taken by surprise and two divisions, with a total of 20,000 men, landed against limited opposition. However, once ashore, the British advance ground to a halt. Turkish reaction was slow, and the key to the operation, which was the high ground, remained unoccupied until the early morning of 9 August. At that crucial point, the Turks occupied it with reinforcements, pre-empting the British who had finally begun to advance. The Suvla operation then degenerated into a repetition of the costly, futile attacks and counter-attacks that characterized earlier operations at Cape Helles and ANZAC Cove.

WEAKNESS OF COMMAND

The failure to exploit was in part a failure of command. The commander of the attacking divisions, Lt Gen Sir Frederick Stopford, was altogether sceptical about the operation and, having had experience of the Western front, was convinced that he needed to wait for substantial artillery to be landed before he could consolidate his position and then conduct a methodical advance. This caution was reinforced by the vague orders he had received, as he had been given latitude over how far and fast he should exploit inland. Under a dynamic commander, this would not have been a problem, but it allowed Stopford to give full play to his natural caution.

Exploitation was also impeded by the difficulty in consolidation. Despite the lack of opposition, the landing quickly degenerated into confusion. This was partly caused by the darkness which caused some of the force to be landed in the wrong place and other men to get lost. Inadequate maps and a breakdown in communications between the various headquarters meant that by dawn the landing force had ceased to function as a single body. The inertia generated by the initial confusion was compounded as the day wore on. Following this, the disembarkation programme broke down, and the discovery of hidden reefs, a sudden thunderstorm and shelling by Turkish forces meant that few supplies and absolutely no artillery were landed on the first day of the landing. The water ships became grounded on the reefs, adding thirst to the landing force's

LEFT: Reinforcements and munitions are landed on ANZAC beach, prior to the Suvla attack. The lack of adequate 'tactical logistical space' is evident, a result of the failure of the April 1915 landings to take the dominating high ground further to the east.

problems of heat and exhaustion. At the end of the first day, the troops had managed to push only 2 miles (3.2km) inland, and the following morning Stopford sent a message to his superior, stating, 'I must now consolidate.'

The failure to exploit at Suvla effectively cost the allies the Gallipoli campaign; they commenced withdrawal in December 1915. The operation well illustrates that amphibious operations are a means to an end and not an end in themselves. The failure to exploit, which stemmed in part from planning and logistic problems – but which was in many respects a command failure – doomed the campaign as whole. It provides a very good example of an operation in which disorganized exploitation proved to be more important than proper consolidation.

CASE STUDY: ANZIO, 1944

Like Suvla, the Allied landings at Anzio, Italy, were an attempt to break a stalemate further south. Like Suvla, the landings succeeded and, like Suvla, lack of exploitation threw away the chance of a major success. Earlier landings at Salerno in southern Italy on 9 September 1943 had gained a firm lodgement and the Allies' next objective was Rome. However, progress from the south was very slow. The German defence, under Field Marshal Albert Kesselring, was skilfully handled, and the terrain was

difficult. By November 1943 the Allied offensive had become mired in a German defensive belt north of Naples which was known as the 'Gustav Line'. It was decided to land two divisions on the west coast of Italy, well behind the German lines; this attack was to be codenamed Operation Shingle.

The landing force was provided by Major General John Lucas's VI Corps, from General Mark Clark's Fifth US Army. The amphibious assault was preceded by diversionary attacks on the Gustav Line which had been designed to draw German troops southwards and away from the Anzio area. Allied intelligence indicated diversionary success and indicated also that the landing area was weakly held. Consequently, the Anzio landings began on 22 January 1944, 33 miles (53km) south of Rome. A total of 378 ships took part and were assisted by massive air support. Landing at night, the lead elements of VI Corps went ashore unopposed and were quickly able to capture Nettuno harbour. Rapid off-loading commenced in the port, enabling 36,000 troops and 3000 vehicles to be landed, all without a casualty.

Frequent air attacks began the day after the landing, on 23 January, and there were also gales. Nevertheless, the process of consolidating the beachhead continued. After a week, nearly 70,000 troops had been positioned ashore and supplies were pouring in. Yet Lucas declined to exploit this opportunity. There were several reasons why. He was a cautious general and his caution was exaggerated by the inherent risks of landing behind the enemy. He was also wary of over-extending himself and of making his force vulnerable to German counter-attack. Furthermore, the orders he had been given were not clear: the operation had been hastily mounted and was something of a compromise between the competing visions of Clark and his superior General Sir Harold Alexander, Commander of 15th Army Group. Lucas therefore received ambiguous orders on what to do once landed. Alexander favoured moving inland and occupying the Alban hills, which would protect the Anzio beachhead and cut the German lines of communication, perhaps managing to unhinge their whole defence. However, Clark favoured

BELOW: A 4.1in (105mm) field howitzer in action in the Nettuno area, Italy, in March 1944. The failure of the Salerno landings to move to the exploitation phase quickly enough allowed the German defenders to seal off the Salerno area. From the Alban hills German artillery was then able to strike the Allied beachhead.

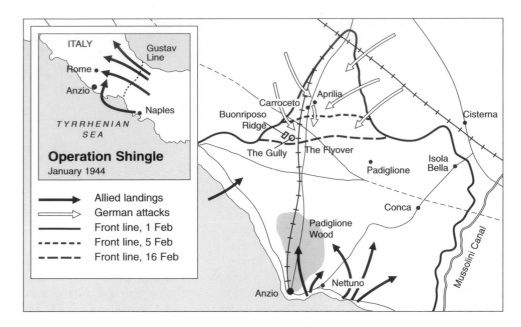

LEFT: The Anzio Beachead, Jan–Feb 1944. Anzio was a classic amphibious turning movement. Although the landing itself was extremely successful, the failure to exploit it rendered the early success irrelevant.

limiting the landing's aim to securing a strong beachhead. Lucas chose the latter strategy, and therefore moved only when reinforcements were imminent. Even then, the advance was slow and methodical, and Lucas took a great deal of care to develop his port and logistical base behind him.

Kesselring was an enterprising and energetic commander. He used Lucas's caution to block the road to Rome and then to mount a counter-attack. By 26 September he had occupied the Alban hills and surrounded the beachhead with six divisions. From the hills, the Germans were able to place observed gunfire onto

LEFT: DUKWs and Allied landing ships at Anzio, 1944. Despite storms, and attacks from German aircraft and glider bombs, the Allies were able to build up their combat power on the beachhead relatively quickly. With the advantage of interior lines of communication and an enterprising commander, however, the Germans were able to shift their forces to the danger area even more rapidly.

ABOVE: German sappers prepare to blow up a bridge to slow down the Allied advance in Italy, 1943. A combination of numerous rivers and high mountains created great problems for the Allied advance. Terrain can prove to be a potent force multiplier for a tactically adept defender.

the Allied beachhead and in this way they inflicted heavy casualties. Allied attempts to push forward also met with serious casualties, and this forced Major General Lucas onto the defensive.

Heavy fighting continued during February as the Germans tried, and failed, to dislodge the Allies. In these battles, the Allies were helped by their intelligence resources – which gave them a picture of the German forces' strength and distribution – and by powerful air and artillery support. Kesselring finally gave up trying to eliminate the Anzio beachhead and instead settled for containing it. The Allied force was trapped there by the Germans for nearly four months and a massive logistic effort was required to keep them supplied with food and ammunition. In the event, it was an offensive from the southern forces that broke the German line and it was not until 25 May 1944 that the Anzio forces managed to link up successfully with the other Allied troops.

Anzio represents the classic use of amphibious forces to turn an enemy's flank. However, in the event, the

operation squandered almost complete tactical surprise by a poor balance between consolidation and exploitation. Lucas's decision not to pursue exploitation was controversial. As it transpired, there were few German forces between Anzio and Rome, and he might well have achieved a resounding success if he had decided to push on quickly. Yet it is difficult not to have some sympathy for the commander. Quick exploitation against a flexible enemy with the advantage of interior lines carried with it the risk of a military disaster that Lucas was unwilling to face. Furthermore, his orders did not explicitly command him to take such a risk.

CASE STUDY: NORMANDY, 1944

The difficulties associated with exploiting an amphibious landing against a tenacious enemy are also demonstrated by the operations in Normandy in 1944. The first part of the battle had been fought on the beach on 6 June. This had gained a lodgement but it had not achieved all of its set objectives. The Allies held a broken front extending 25 miles (40km) across

LEFT: American troops crammed into a LCT on the way to France. Despite facing a determined and skilful defensive campaign in Normandy, the Allies were still able to triumph. This was due in no small measure to their ability to continuously reinforce the Normandy beachheads without serious interruption by the Germans.

and less than 5 miles (8km) in depth. The battle had to continue if the Allies wished to avoid being hemmed in, as they had been at Anzio.

Consolidation of the landing proceeded reasonably well. The massive influx of men, vehicles and matériel continued without major interruption by the Germans. However, utilizing these forces to effect a dramatic breakout was more difficult and the prospects for a quick breakthrough were not realized. Subsequent attempts to exploit the landings showed the difficulty in pursuing an advance against a determined foe without the benefit of surprise, even

though the Allies enjoyed massive air, artillery and logistics superiority. Counter-attacks against the Allied bridgehead were launched by 21st Panzer Division and 12th SS Panzer Division and the German forces succeeded in establishing a defence line around the Allied beachhead. On 25 July, 49 days after the landing, the Allies held positions which they had previously hoped they would be able to take within 15 days.

In exploiting their landings, the Allies faced a number of difficulties. The terrain in Normandy was well suited for the defence. Known as 'bocage', this land consisted of small fields, sunken roads,

LEFT: Allied infantry fighting amongst the Bocage countryside. The difficult terrain beyond the Normandy beachheads negated many of the advantages held by the Allies and dramatically slowed the process of exploitation.

woods and high hedges, all of which conspired to impede mobility and channel attacks onto a narrow frontage. Tanks, in which the Allies had a significant superiority in numbers, were made much less useful in the bocage than the infantry, which was forced to bear the brunt of the wearying, close-range fighting. There was a near equivalence of the numbers in infantry on each side during the initial stages but the Germans proved to be tactically adept in the defence. In addition to the skills of their troops, the Germans possessed excellent anti-tank weapons such as the *panzerfaust*. Although Allied airpower disrupted the movement of German troops, expedients such as good use of camouflage, deployment close to Allied forces and

night movement prevented this advantage from becoming overwhelming. By 9 June, a continuous front had been formed from the Allied beachheads; however, its expansion was to proceed at a painfully slow pace.

In the east of the bridgehead, which was occupied by the British and Canadians of 21st Army group, activity was focused on taking the town of Caen. Caen was a major nodal point, and beyond this town lay open ground over which the Allies could use their superiority in tanks. Field Marshal Montgomery, commander of 21st Army Group, first sought to take Caen by direct assaults on the night of 7/8 June. The failure of these assaults prompted Montgomery to attempt to outflank Caen, but his attempts were halted with heavy casualties. On 17 July another operation, named Goodwood, was initiated. Three armoured divisions of VIII Corps were sent into the attack; they were preceded by an enormous air bombardment by 1000 bombers and heavy NGS support. However, the German defences were 8 miles (13km) deep and the bombardment had less effect than had been predicted. German losses were heavy but an Allied breakthrough was not attained. By 20 July, Goodwood was over.

One positive result of Operation Goodwood for the British and Canadian troops was that their efforts drew German reserves eastwards. With the defences in front of them thinned, US forces were able to achieve a breakthrough. After hard fighting, the port of Cherbourg was taken on 27 June. Further severe fighting ensued, in which VIII Corps lost 10,000 men in 12 days for a gain of only 7 miles (11.2km). The assault finally yielded the town of St Lô by 20 July. On 25 July the US forces launched Operation Cobra, an attack on a narrow front that broke the overstretched German defences, and Avranches was reached on 30 July. Patton's newly created 3rd Army then quickly pushed forward. German counter-attacks on 6 August were ravaged by air attacks and beaten back, and the Allies began to encircle them. As US forces pushed east, British and Canadians pushed south in Operation Totalize and Tractable, reaching within 1 mile (1.6km) of Falaise on 15 August. The German 7th Army and 5th Panzer Army were now in

BELOW: A German 4.1in (105mm) howitzer set up in the streets of Cherbourg during heavy fighting for the city in June 1944. Cherbourg fell six weeks later than scheduled, despite Allied advantages such as almost complete air superiority.

LEFT: Two Canadian soldiers search out Germans left behind in a village captured during the advance on Falaise, 12 August 1944. Exploitation often poses a dilemma; should the advancing forces pause to 'mop up' all the remaining defenders, consolidating their position at the risk of losing momentum, or should they push on regardless, accepting the risk posed by such forces to their flank and rear?

a salient from which they attempted to withdraw, suffering heavily. The battle for Normandy was effectively over by 15 August when Falaise fell, and on 25 August the French capital, Paris, was liberated. The campaign as a whole had cost the Allies 209,000 casualties as opposed to German losses of 440,000.

Overlord demonstrated the importance of continuous reinforcement of the beachhead, a function of continued Allied superiority in the air and on the sea. Even as exploitation was under way, the build-up of combat power behind the front line continued. On the eve of Operation Cobra, within the 1570 sq. miles (4066 sq. km) which the Allies had managed to occupy were 36 allied divisions, totalling around one and a half million men. US forces alone, consisting of 19 divisions, were being supplied with 22,000 tonnes of supplies a day. The Allies' ability to continue to funnel troops and supplies

through the beachhead allowed them to stretch the German defence until it eventually broke.

CONCLUSION

The consolidation and exploitation phases of an amphibious assault are often vital to the overall success – or failure – of an operation. A period of consolidation is necessary to expand the beachhead to an adequate size, to secure it against enemy attack, and to develop the combat power, logistic support, and command and control which is necessary for a breakout and the attainment of higher-level objectives. Yet the time spent consolidating has to be balanced by the need to exploit the success of the amphibious landing. Without such exploitation, the initiative may be lost to the enemy who, using internal lines, may be able to consolidate its position and then counter-attack.

CHAPTER SIX

LOGISTICS

Logistics is the *sine qua non* of military operations. Without proper organization and supply, few amphibious assaults succeed.

Logistics can be defined as the practical art of moving armed forces and keeping them supplied. It is a vital part of any military operation, and, as Napoleon commented, 'Victory goes to the side that knows how to concentrate the largest number of troops at the decisive point.' It is true of amphibious operations, as of all military enterprises, that success depends not only on numbers, technology and experience but also on factors such as administration, transportation, communication and supply. Forces must be assembled; troops must be moved; and rations, ammunition, fuel and stores must be delivered on time and also in the right sequence in order to enable operations to continue. As supplies move forward, arrangements also need to be made for casualties, empty supply vessels and prisoners-of-war, as well as for damaged equipment to pass back down the lines of communication. The inadequate provision of logistic support will prove to affect the tempo, direction and intensity of operations and later may have disastrous consequences.

In amphibious operations, the functions of logistics include embarkation, movement to the objective area, the disembarkation of personnel and the unloading of ships, as well as the provision of supply, medical, salvage, evacuation, construction, repair and maintenance services. An important feature of amphibious logistics is that the logistic support travels with the amphibious task force. This creates certain advantages in mobility and flexibility over land-based logistic structures. However, it can also generate some difficulties.

LEFT: Supply parties transfer critical stores across the beaches of Iwo Jima, 21 February 1945. At Iwo Jima, US logistics ashore was helped by the small size of the island, but in other campaigns, such as Gallipoli, logistic bottlenecks at the beach have translated into difficulties at the front.

ABOVE: Troops of the Eighth Army embark on Landing Craft Infantry (LCI) at a North African port en route to Sicily. Specialist equipment such as the LCI confer many advantages. The infantry loaded here can disembark straight onto the beach in the objective area, greatly simplifying the process of moving both troops and supplies ashore.

Land operations will generally have a period of preparation in which to build up the logistic support for an attack. In contrast to this, amphibious logistics depend upon securing a beachhead and offloading into an often hostile environment. Logistic development proceeds in parallel with the assault, rather than preceding the assault.

LOGISTIC PLANNING

Logistic planning is a command responsibility and involves the amphibious task force commander in addition to his landing and naval force subordinates. The amphibious logistic plan needs to be comprehensive and to address such tasks as: preparing embarkation schedules; assembling shipping at embarkation points, organizing the logistic shipping; and providing the means to establish and maintain an adequate supply system in the objective area, in addition to developing the plans for dealing with prisoners and the reception of casualties. The logistic plan needs to ensure not only that the landing force can be taken to the objective area but also that the means are available to support it in the assault, consolidation and exploitation phases of the operation. Because of the peculiar challenges of amphibious logistics, the main part of the logistic organization is provided by specialist personnel who control the offloading of ships, run the logistics operations centre and coordinate details ashore. They are responsible for commanding and manning base areas, as well as providing second-line transport.

One of the difficulties with logistic planning is that the range of factors that inform planning is wide. Logistic preparation takes into account the character, size and duration of the intended operation; the target date, which will affect such things as the time available for planning and weather conditions; the characteristics of the objective area, such as beach conditions and the availability of ports; enemy capabilities, in particular the ability to attack friendly logistic lines; and the strength and composition of the landing force, which will influence the quantity and types of supplies which are required. Further considerations might include the logistic capabilities of the landing force itself, which will influence the amount and longevity of sea-based support; the scale of the logistics means available, such as the number of helicopters or trucks; and also the quality of the communications systems available, which will have an influence on the ability to coordinate and control the logistics efforts. Ultimately, many of the factors that support logistic planning are subjective assessments. Often it is only the acid test of the amphibious operation itself that will be able to reveal the enemy

capabilities, the rate of usage of supplies by the landing force, or the amount of supply that the logistic system can deliver. However, in making such judgments, the training and experience of logistic personnel is paramount.

Another requirement for successful logistic planning is the close cooperation between logistic and operations staff; it is essential that the two work in harmony in order to ensure that the logistic plan is fully integrated into the operational plan as a whole. Logistic considerations – such as the need to seize enemy ports quickly – may influence the assault plan, just as the requirements of the assault – such as the need to move quickly off the beach – may have implications for the logistic plan. Once the integrated plan is developed, the performance of the logistic parts can be improved by conducting rehearsals.

There are certain tensions inherent in the planning process, which are caused by the need to balance advance planning with a certain flexibility. Since 'no plan survives contact with the enemy', flexibility needs to be built into logistic

BELOW: Italian prisoners of war unload the British freighter *Ulla* at Palermo. Large amphibious assaults will often eventually require the capture of a deep-water port if logistic throughput is to be maintained. Amphibious plans must take into account logistic considerations when the objectives for an operation are being framed.

BELOW: Crewmen from an American escort carrier handle supplies on their ship's forward flight decks in Kerama-retto anchorage, near Okinawa, April 1945. Without an extensive fleet train to bring such supplies forward, the US island-hopping campaign would have been severely curtailed.

planning in order to take into account changing circumstances, to remedy unexpected problems or to exploit unforeseen opportunities. Yet creating a viable logistic framework often requires detailed preparation, timetables and coordination of different echelons and this can result in a certain rigidity in execution. Moreover, there is not necessarily a relationship between the amount of preparation time involved in planning for a campaign and its eventual success; there are many instances of success that has been achieved by hurriedly

mounted operations. For example, the US assault on Guadalcanal was launched in a relatively short space of time without the usual preparation and rehearsal, and this led to it to being given the nickname Operation Shoestring. Therefore, it is the quality of the logistic planning, founded upon the accuracy of its fundamental assumptions, rather than the quantity of planning, which is the key to success.

EMBARKATION AND TRANSIT

At every stage of an amphibious operation, logistic factors are considered.

Some of these factors are detailed here.

The embarkation phase provides for the orderly assembly and embarkation of personnel and equipment. This is carried out in a sequence which is designed to mirror the order in which the personnel and equipment will be required when they land. This is often termed 'tactical' or 'combat' loading. The principles of tactical loading run counter to normal naval loading practice, since with tactical loading often the heaviest equipment – such as vehicles – is on deck, and the lighter equipment is in the hold. Under-loading is also necessary to allow space for loads to be manipulated if circumstances later force a change in the disembarkation priorities. Ideally, each load should be autonomous, so that the force in each ship can be self-sufficient for the assault phase; this means that the loss of one ship in the fleet will not cripple the whole force. In the Gallipoli campaign in 1915, the invasion force was not initially tactically loaded; for example, the artillery was in one ship but the limbers to move them were on another

ship. Moreover, the nearest harbour to the objective area – Mudros harbour on Lemnos – did not have either the wharves or the heavy equipment to enable reloading, so that the entire force had to move on to Alexandria in Egypt. Naturally, this greatly delayed the operation. Tactical loading is always made much easier if the amphibious commander has a very clear idea of what his mission will be in the objective area. He can then tailor the tactical

ABOVE: A truck from the US Army Medical Corps exits an LST (Landing Ship Tank) via a landing ramp made up of a Rhino ferry.

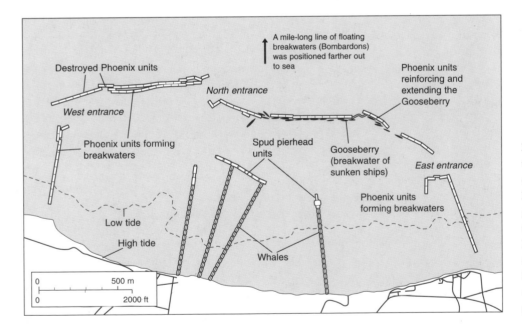

LEFT AND BELOW: Although they performed less well than expected, the Mulberry harbours at Normandy did give the Allies confidence at the planning stage that the logistic challenges posed by the Normandy landings could be overcome. They therefore contributed to the decision to go ahead with the invasion.

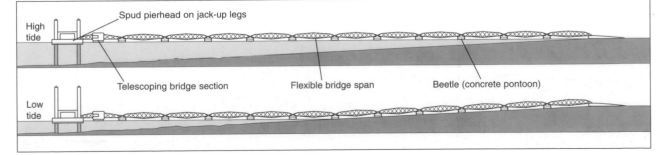

ABOVE: Troops come ashore at Leyte, in the Philippines. Here a member of the Beach Party holds a beach marker, designed to guide landing craft onto a designated sector of the shore. Specialist logistic personnel are a great advantage in organizing and implementing a smooth flow of supplies and matériel through the beachhead.

loading to a specific plan of assault.

During the passage to the objective, depending upon the distances travelled, the amphibious force may have to arrange logistics support for what is called Replenishment At Sea (RAS). Fuel taken aboard from tankers is likely to be the main element needed at this point in the proceedings. En route to the objective area, a halt may also be taken. This is taken for several reasons: to give an opportunity to resupply the amphibious force; to alter the tactical loading of ships; or to rehearse routines, such as disembarkation. The availability of bases and/or pre-positioned logistic stocks such as Maritime Pre-Positioning Ships (MPS) – as were used by the USA in the Gulf – serves to help the logistic situation considerably.

LANDING AND OFFLOADING

The ship-to-shore movement plan is another logistic factor which needs to be taken into consideration. In the objective area, it will be necessary for the staff of the amphibious task group to consider the logistic unloading plan. Logistic personnel who know where the supplies are within the fleet will remain afloat, whereas all other personnel will move

ashore at the point when the landing force commander shifts his headquarters. The ship-to-shore movement plan will need to choose the best mix of assets and routes to move supplies. Helicopters are quick, but their loads can vary in size. Landing craft, rafts, boats, amphibians and pontoons are likely to be the main means of transferring men and supplies ashore. As with amphibious transport, ship-to-shore movement is eased considerably by the use of specialist equipment. Consideration needs to be given to whether to beach large ships, such as LSTs. This can reduce offload times by a factor of seven but it may also make them more vulnerable. The pace of the logistic offload is also critical. Operation Sealion was cancelled primarily because of the inability of the Germans to gain sea control, but it was also due to their logistic problems; despite having assembled 168 steamers, 1900 barges, 221 tugs and 1000 smaller craft, it would still have required days to land the first wave. As well as specialist shipping, specialist personnel contribute to the success of ship-to-shore movement. At the Fedala landings of Operation Torch, 18 of the 25 landing craft present in the first wave were wrecked in the approach. This was primarily because inexperienced crews could not cope with the heavy seas.

Another logistic factor to consider is that of landing. The first logistic offload is likely to be first-line combat supplies (ammunition, rations and fuel) plus medical and repair teams. A general offload of personnel and matériel begins once the beachhead has been established and fighting has moved inland. In order that the logistics moved ashore can be quickly utilized by the landing force, a logistic landing force is sent ashore in order to organize the beach to receive, store and distribute supplies. This might consist of a headquarters, a helicopter support group and one or two shore party groups. Beaching points are marked to direct landing craft ashore. Stores dumps are then marked out in order to establish areas within which to reorganize and store supplies. Distribution points are established, from which supplies are drawn by the landing force. The beaches may be prepared with tracking to firm it up and routes off the beach may be marked. The amphibious force's ability to develop its logistic base ashore will depend upon many factors. The availability of local facilities such as ports or airfields is often a significant help. Experienced logistic personnel will also be a benefit to the process; at Guadalcanal, inexperience in unloading practices helped to slow down the logistic offload.

SUSTAINED SUPPORT

In its initial stages, the landing force relies on the amphibious task force shipping for continuing and coordinated logistic and administrative support. As the landing is consolidated, a decision is taken about the amount of logistic support that will be brought ashore. The operation may adopt the traditional shore-based approach, in which logistic support is moved as quickly as possible to the shore. On or near the best beach or in a port, a main support area is established; this is then used to build up large stores dumps, bulk fuel installations, a field dressing station and a forward operating area for helicopters, as well as maintenance and repair facilities. The support area may also act as a holding area for reinforcements and prisoners. As it is a prime target, such a support area needs protection by

friendly forces and through dispersal and camouflage. An alternative is to conduct a partial offload; immediate replenishment is disembarked to sustain the assaulting units and some detachments are also sent ashore, including forward repair teams, and medical and ammunition control groups. However, the bulk of the supplies are kept at sea. The remaining option is sea-basing, in which almost all of the logistic support remains afloat, with the movement of supplies controlled by the logistic landing party. This avoids the establishment of large logistic bases ashore with their associated protection requirements and also gives maximum logistic flexibility and mobility. Sea-based logistics is a vital part of the evolving concept of Ship To Objective Manoeuvre (STOM). However, it requires good logistic efficiency and management, and also concentrates the landing force's supplies in a relatively small number of potentially vulnerable ships. It remains to be seen whether this demanding logistic strategy can be made fully effective.

Another consideration when looking at logistics is exploitation. The advance from the beachhead requires a firm logistic base. As the attack moves forward and both logistic consumption and lines of supply increase, the transport and beach facilities must be adequate for the necessary logistics to move through the beach to the front line. One of the major bottlenecks at Tarawa was the logistic support. Enemy resistance and in-adequacies in shore control meant that

BELOW: The US invasion fleet stands off the island of Okinawa, two days after the landings. The vast size of the fleets required for the US island-hopping campaign is evident. The airfield of Yon Tan is left centre; this fell on the first day of the invasion. However, aircraft could not hope to provide the necessary logistic support for the fleet.

ABOVE: Construction of the Mulberry harbours off the Normandy coast, 1944. Their main enemy proved to be the weather. If the Germans had been able to contest Allied air superiority more effectively, however, the harbours would have been extremely vulnerable.

the supplies on Betio were inadequate. By the time of the Iwo Jima landing they were much improved, with the troops even receiving mail during the first month of the campaign.

There are other considerations to take into account. Protecting the amphibious force's logistic structures is vital. If Sea Lines of Communication (SLOCs) are cut by the enemy, or if critical logistic assets are destroyed during unloading, the viability of the whole operation may be threatened. Where sea control has not been attained, logistic lines can be very vulnerable; in fact, this was one of the great risks of the German invasion of Norway in April 1940. The potential for a wider disaster was illustrated by the attack on Narvik when, after the initial attack had been carried out, one of the two tankers sent to refuel the naval flotilla was intercepted. This also happened to two of the three steamers of the troops' transport group which were carrying equipment and supplies.

CASE STUDY: NORMANDY, 1944

Logistic considerations were central to Operation Overlord. Allied military success of this operation depended upon the Allies being able to build up a matériel superiority at the landing sites before the major German reinforcements could arrive. This in turn depended on being able to establish a sustainable, high-capacity logistic line across the Channel. It also required measures to attack the

German logistic system and thereby undermine their capabilities.

Detailed planning went into trying to identify the critical factors that would influence logistics on the day. These were deemed to be: the number of landing craft and transports available; the size and number of the beaches; prevailing weather conditions; access inland; the availability of deep-water ports; and the feasibility of providing air support to protect the landing and hamper the enemy. These factors would influence the quantity of logistic offload that could be conducted, and the speed with which it could be carried out. A detailed logistic plan was then set out for the first 90 days: how many troops would be landed; when; where; and in what order. Procedures were set in place for clearing and operating the beach. establishing supply dumps, and unloading transports, as well as for requisitioning, packing and forwarding items from the beach to the troops. Plans were drawn up for the repair and restoration of the ports that were to be captured, such as Cherbourg. Logistic factors had an important bearing on all aspects of the operation. For example, the rationale for the landing at Utah beach was to facilitate the capture of Cherbourg in order that a deep-water port could be used as early as possible.

Time and the operation's priority in terms of resources allow the creation of tailored solutions to some logistic problems. The raid on Dieppe in 1942

had shown the difficulty of taking a port by direct assault, so portable harbours, which were known as Mulberries, were developed. Each harbour, consisting of blockships, concrete caissons and floating piers and roadways, was expected to have the capacity to unload 6000 tonnes of stores a day. They were towed across the Channel after the assault and assembled offshore. One Mulberry harbour was deployed at St Laurent for US troops and the other was deployed at Arromanches for the British and Canadians. The first ship unloaded at a Mulberry on 14 June. Another innovation was PLUTO – the Pipe Line Under The Ocean – which was a flexible pipe running from the Isle of Wight to Cherbourg and pumping petrol directly into fuel depots in France. Later pipelines were run from the south coast of Kent to Boulogne. Buoyed pipelines were also developed and these allowed tankers offshore to pump petrol directly to storage tanks ashore.

In addition to being informed by the Allies and considerable experience of amphibious logistics, success at Normandy also derived from effective preparation. Intensive training and practice was conducted in tactical loading, ship-to-shore movement, beach party operations, beach marking, salvage and maintenance. Boat crews practised disembarkation of men and supplies

ABOVE: Reinforcements are brought on to Utah beach on board a Coast Guard manned landing craft. In the background is a Rhino ferry carrying ambulances.

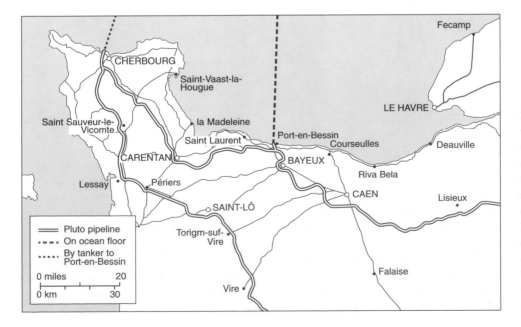

LEFT: The Allies deployed vast numbers of vehicles in their invasion of Europe and, if the momentum of the offensive was to be maintained, these had to be supplied with abundant fuel. PLUTO was an innovative attempt to deliver fuel directly across the Channel, but, like the Mulberries, it was much less effective than anticipated.

including beaching, unloading and retracting. Major exercises were conducted; one such example was the large Fabius I exercise of 3–6 May which involved the complete unloading of the participating ships. Efforts were made to improve existing equipment; many LSTs were given better communications, vehicle-loading and mooring facilities. In order to help land stores, Rhino ferries were created by attaching engines to rafts made from pontoons which had been lashed together.

Success was also achieved despite the rapid breakdown of the logistic plans in the face of heavy surf and enemy resistance. The progress in clearing beaches was slow, so the beachhead area became congested. A severe storm blew up between 19 and 22 June, sinking many craft and severely delaying unloading. The total number of supplies landed per day fell from 24,000 tonnes to only 4500 tonnes. The US Mulberry was quickly swamped by the storm and was destroyed

but the UK Mulberry survived and was repaired using remnants of the American harbour. By early July, it was discharging 7000 tonnes a day in addition to 45,000 tonnes that were landed directly over the beach in the US and UK sectors. Nevertheless, problems still persisted. The deep-water port of Cherbourg was captured later than expected, and the Germans had deliberately destroyed its facilities. Because of this, Cherbourg began operation six weeks behind schedule; even then, it operated well below the anticipated capacity. In June the total US supplies received were less than 75 per cent of those anticipated, thus inhibiting offensive operations.

Some of the difficulties were caused by the rigidity of the plans. By trying to create timetables that provided maximum theoretical efficiency, the planners had failed to take into account the inevitable delays, uncertainties and frictions of war. Thus, the attempt to keep to unloading schedules led to confusion, and this had a

BELOW: Manned by members of the US Coast Guard, LSTs utilize sandbag piers in order to to disgorge their cargo at Leyte in the Philippines. One important logistic consideration is what proportion of the amphibious force's logistic support should be landed and what should remain afloat.

LEFT: Fuel and water drums crowd a Guadalcanal beach during large-scale Marine manoeuvres, 18 May 1944. US logistics was made much easier by US command of the sea and air; this allowed concentrated logistic dumps to be built up without serious interference from the enemy.

ripple effect along the whole logistic chain, for example, upsetting timetables for reloading returning ships. Ultimately, the logistic chain survived because ad-hoc solutions drastically increased the quantity of supplies which could be delivered at the beaches. For example, the Navy began to leave landing ships and coasters dried out on the beach at low tide, allowing supplies to be delivered straight onto the shore rather than via pontoon piers. The supply situation was also helped by the slowness of the initial advance, as this cut down on fuel requirements and kept the logistic chain short. Allied air superiority and sea control also prevented the Germans from seriously interfering with the beachheads, speeding up disembarkation and allowing supplies to be piled onto the cramped beachheads, often uncamouflaged.

Despite the continued pessimism of logistic personnel, Operation Overlord received enough logistic support to enable consolidation and exploitation to occur. Although in September 1944 there were difficulties in getting supplies forward, which caused a temporary halt in the advance, the critical phase of the campaign was now over; the troops were ashore, and they were staying ashore. Logistically, then, Normandy was a triumph of planning, supported on the day by improvisation which had been informed by experience.

CASE STUDY: THE PACIFIC CAMPAIGN, 1942–5

The logistic challenges imposed by the US 'island-hopping' campaign across the Pacific were formidable. Lines of communications stretched thousands of miles across the ocean. The operations which were undertaken were in fact major amphibious assaults. Large forces of ships and personnel had to be sustained in the advance to the objective area, as well as be kept in forward positions for extended periods. These cross-Pacific logistic problems went well beyond pre-war US experience and planning.

The scale of the logistic task was illustrated by the operations in the Marianas in 1944, which included the attacks on Guam, Tinian and Saipan. These were huge and enormously complex operations. One of the two corps assigned to the operation had to be brought from Hawaii and the western United States; another corps had to be brought from Guadalcanal. From throughout the Pacific, the ships intended to be used for the invasion were assembled at the Marshall Islands in a specific order and at a specific time in order to enable tactical loading and the dispatch of shipping echelons in the appropriate sequence. The shipping then had to move, according to a careful timetable, to a target 1000 miles (1600km) away. The force allocated to

ABOVE: Yellow Beach, Okinawa. Chaos seems to reign as ships, supplies, equipment and men crowd the shore area. However, in reality, the beach was carefully organized.

BELOW: An ammunition ship transfers bombs to the USS *Randolph* while in the Pacific. Replenishment at sea can drastically increase the range at which amphibious operations can be conducted.

the campaign included 106,000 troops and 535 ships, and the troops were allotted 32 days of rations and 20 days of other supplies. The northern half of the attack force alone had to load 75,000 tonnes of cargo, totalling 8 million cubic feet (226,354 cubic metres). The fleet then had to organize a rendezvous at Eniwetok on 8 June to carry out final preparations for the attack.

A prerequisite for the success of these operations was the development of a mobile logistic system, which was based upon an enormous assemblage of logistic ships, termed a 'fleet train'. After the Pacific War, the flexibility to be gained from a comprehensive fleet train was recognized, and it became an essential component of all US amphibious operations. For the first part of the war, logistic support for the amphibious fleet was shore-based. These bases were established in advanced areas, such as Espiritu Santo, Manus and Guadalcanal, and incorporated storage, repair and maintenance facilities, as well as harbour defences. The difficulty with shore-based logistic support was that the nature of the amphibious campaign was dynamic, with the island-hopping campaigns pushing forward over large distances. Shore-based facilities, on the other hand, were static and shifting them forward was a slow process. It also absorbed large numbers of transport ships and other craft such as LSTs, reducing the numbers available for offensive amphibious operations. There-fore, from the capture of the Marshall Islands in 1944, supported by a huge US ship-building programme, afloat logistics became the dominant form of logistic support. The US Fifth Fleet organized its logistic ships into Service Squadron Ten. This squadron consisted of repair ships, floating dry docks, ammunition ships, hospital ships, fuel tankers, water-distillation vessels, survey ships and floating barracks. The immense resources possessed by the USA allowed it to generate an unprecedented level of afloat support, including the Advanced Base Sectional Dock (ABSD) which was capable of docking even the largest amphibious ship.

These ships could be brought together at anchorages to provide what were, in effect, floating bases. Examples of these include the bases established at Samar near the Philippines and those near Okinawa. For the latter, the island of Kerama-retto was occupied prior to the assault as a harbour for the logistic ships. Floating bases were also capable of operating without proximity to land, although deployment near to land carried the advantage of land-based air support. Floating bases allowed the USA to operate a sea-based logistics strategy for its landings, maintaining the bulk of supplies afloat until needed ashore. In doing this, they gained important advantages in terms of mobility and flexibility in their operations ashore.

The fleet train was also vital in providing support to the ships within the amphibious forces. Replenishment by the fleet train allowed amphibious ships to remain at sea for extended periods of time. One major requirement was fuel oil, and the tankers of the fleet train enabled ships to be refuelled every three to five days with the tanker and warship sailing in proximity while the fuel was being delivered through a hose. Ammunition was another critical need and here replenishment capability at sea had the advantage that less of this bulky commodity had to be carried by warships. Transfers between ships were also extended to include personnel and aircraft. For operations at Okinawa, for example, the replenishment force consisted of 16 tankers, four ammunition ships, tugs and salvage vessels, aircraft transports and supply ships which were all protected by an escort.

The significance of the enormous US fleet train is evident when it is compared with the British experience in the Pacific. Task Force 57 – the British Pacific Fleet established in 1944 – found the scope of its operations severely curtailed by its inadequate mobile logistic capability. The Admiralty received only 293,000 tonnes of shipping for Task Force 57's fleet train, instead of the estimated one to one and a half million tonnes and at least 95 ships that had been requested. The fleet therefore continued to rely on supply drawn from a fleet base in Australia and an advanced base established in the Pacific. This created great difficulties in cooperation between the British and US fleets, as the latter possessed much better mobility, sustainability and force-projection capability.

CASE STUDY: THE FALKLANDS CAMPAIGN, 1982

With a supply line of 8000 miles (12,870km), logistics inevitably cast a heavy shadow over British efforts to retake the Falkland Islands. Of more than 100 ships which were deployed in Operation Corporate, 25 were Royal Fleet Auxiliaries (RFAs, support ships manned by the merchant navy, but trained and equipped to meet Royal Navy needs), and 45 were STUFT. The STUFT ships were vital in meeting logistic needs in a range of roles that could not be met by the Navy, including troop transports (the liners *Canberra* and *QE2*); aircraft ferries (the container ship *Atlantic Conveyor*); supply ships (the freighters *Lycaon* and *Saxonia*); hospital ships (the liner *Uganda*); and tankers. Some air supply was also available and several Hercules C-130s sorties were undertaken in order to parachute in specialist supplies and personnel.

Perhaps one of the longest-running logistic problems which occurred during the Falklands campaign was that of tactical loading. Proper tactical loading proved to be difficult to conduct. The fluid political situation during the early days of the crisis meant a combination of pressure to sail quickly, a lack of clarity about the amphibious force's exact

BELOW: The P&O Ferry *Elk* en route to the Falklands, with equipment on deck. STUFT were absolutely essential to the logistic dimensions of the British campaign, making up nearly half of the total fleet sent. They provided everything from ammunition carriers to troop transports.

mission and the addition of new forces, all of which upset preceding logistic plans. Thus supplies tended to be loaded as they appeared at the docks, and on 14 April a whole new brigade was added to the landing force, thereby doubling its size. A re-stow was undertaken at Ascension, but this was hampered by the lack of facilities on the island. Despite attempts at 'cross-decking' (moving supplies between ships by helicopter), the loading of the force was far from ideal and this meant that offloading in the objective area would also be problematic.

However, the force did have the benefit of embarked logistic specialists, the Commando Logistic Regiment. The British also had access to much local knowledge on airfields, climate, the road system, fuel and food stocks. However, the additional brigade which was embarked on 14 April did not have its own logistic regiment. The Commando Logistic Regiment, which had been established to support around 3000 troops, ended up supporting a division of more than 8000. En route the task force was sustained through Replenishment at Sea (RAS) from tankers but this was far

from easy since the seas were often rough. Water was also a problem; it was overcome on the roll-on, roll-off ferries by loading water bowsers onto the car decks, and on others by fitting reverse osmosis equipment before embarkation.

In the landing area, a number of factors affected the logistic offload. Without tactical loading, a well-regulated disembarkation was not possible and there was much improvisation on the day. This difficulty was compounded by the shortage of ship-to-shore transport. The British relied on Landing Craft, Utility (LCUs) which were capable of carrying two light tanks or 200 men or 100 tonnes of supplies, and Landing Craft, Vehicle and Personnel (LCVPs) capable of carrying 30 men or a small vehicle and a trailer. Fortunately for the British, some of the RFAs were Landing Ships, Logistics (LSLs). Given the right conditions, these ships could land their cargo directly onto the beach. Mexeflotes were also available: these were large pontoon rafts powered by large outboard motors which were capable of carrying 60 tonnes. The landing ships *Fearless* and *Intrepid* carried only four LCUs and four

BELOW: British troops load their one surviving Chinook heavy-lift helicopter. The Falklands had few roads and plenty of very poor terrain, making helicopters crucial to the logistic sustainment of the British advance. Even so, with too few helicopters to perform all the required tasks, the bulk of the infantry were still required to march on foot the 60 miles (96km) to Port Stanley.

LCVPs each, and there were three Mexeflotes. There was also a distinct shortage of helicopters.

Argentine opposition was also a factor which affected the logistics. The vulnerability of the logistic effort was illustrated on 25 May when an Argentine Exocet sank the *Atlantic Conveyor*, which was at that time carrying three of the four Chinook heavy lift helicopters and six Wessex helicopters. Any hope of a fast advance of the ground force by helicopter 'hops' was consequently crushed; instead, the bulk of the infantry were forced to march with an average load of 120lb (54kg) of equipment over poor terrain and into contact with enemy forces. The *Atlantic Conveyor* also sank with the landing force's stock of tents. The damage from Argentine air attack would have been much worse if, in the initial stages, their pilots had focused on logistic ships rather than warships; this was a significant error on their part. The continued Argentine air attacks influenced the British offload strategy. Sea-basing was considered too dangerous without complete sea control, so attempts were made to get as much of the logistic support ashore as possible. It was also decided to move some vulnerable ships out of the objective area, even before they were completely unloaded; the *Canberra*, known as the 'Great White Whale', left with 90,000 man-days of rations – as well as much of the first line stores – still aboard. This meant that the logistic regiment had to begin to support the landing force immediately, instead of after the customary 48 hours.

Despite these problems, a support area was established ashore and 32,000 tonnes of supplies were offloaded. Engineers assembled matting to allow Harriers to operate ashore and the build-up of forces ashore began. The period of logistic consolidation was cut short after the landing force commander was ordered forward by the British Government, which was fearful of the UN imposing a ceasefire. Despite this, logistic support was sufficient for the exploitation of the landing – if only just. In addition to the terrain and weather, the shortage in airlift capability was still a major problem. The provision of ammunition for artillery was a particular difficulty; it took 60 Sea

King helicopter sorties to move 480 artillery shells. In the attack on Mt Harriet alone, a total of 3000 rounds were fired off.

The successful logistic support of Operation Corporate was a prodigious feat; 28,000 men and over 100 ships were supplied in a combat zone at a distance of 8000 miles (12,870km) from the home base. Nevertheless, as with the operation as a whole, it was a close-run thing.

ABOVE: The *Atlantic Conveyor* after being hit by an Exocet missile. STUFT ships can be extremely vulnerable, as they are not designed for the rigours of combat. Had the Argentine Airforce targeted the logistic component of the British task force instead of the warships, they might have inflicted decisive losses.

CONCLUSION

Logistics are often ignored in accounts of amphibious campaigns. This is a major oversight, since they are crucial elements of landing operations and have a bearing on every stage of an amphibious campaign, from inception to exploitation. If insufficient attention is paid to issues such as organization, administration and supply, the assault will be greatly complicated or may even fail completely. While the basics of amphibious logistics are relatively simple (move the amphibious force to the objective area, organize storage afloat, organize storage on the beach, and organize a system of movement between the two), putting them in place relies on a combination of sound planning, experience and adequate resources. Moreover, whatever the theory of good logistics may attempt to impose on the practice of operations, the actuality of war has a habit of upsetting even the most well-conceived logistic systems.

CHAPTER SEVEN

AMPHIBIOUS WITHDRAWALS

The ability to withdraw equipment and personnel by sea can be vital in preventing a defeat on land becoming a disaster.

One of the most important tasks to be performed by an amphibious force is the withdrawal of friendly combatants or non-combatants in naval ships, craft or helicopters. This process is undertaken in order to remove them from potential danger ashore. In the case of fighting forces, the purpose of the withdrawal may be to remove troops and equipment from the danger posed by superior enemy forces, thus saving them from capture and enabling them to fight another day. This may be pre-planned as the final stage of an amphibious raid, or it may occur unexpectedly as a result of enemy activity. If it is the result of enemy activity, then the withdrawal is likely to occur at short notice and may have to take place without the benefit of conventional port facilities or even specialist amphibious shipping. Withdrawals are often conducted within range of enemy land, sea and air forces and may occur at a time when friendly forces have been degraded by enemy action. As such, amphibious withdrawals can be amongst the most difficult and dangerous of all military activities. They tend to receive less publicity than assault landings, perhaps for obvious reasons, and they are more often associated with defeat than with victory. However, in saving personnel

LEFT: The evacuation of Gallipoli; stores and transports are loaded at Helles Bay. Ironically, the withdrawal was the most successful operation undertaken during the campaign. Despite the extraordinary difficulty of the task, more than 120,000 men were evacuated from the beachheads. Early assessments of likely casualties ranged as high as 50 per cent losses, but, in the event, casualties were minimal.

RIGHT: A Lockheed C-141 Starlifter. The Starlifter is a capable aircraft, able to carry either 200 troops or 68,340lb (31,000kg) of cargo. Its in-flight refuelling capability gives it an enormous range. Even so, sea lift remains the most effective way of moving large bodies of troops, heavy equipment and cargo.

and material from potential capture or destruction, amphibious withdrawals are processes which offer a unique and sometimes vital capability.

Withdrawals can be conducted by conventional fixed-wing aircraft, provided that secure airfield facilities are available and that enemy fighters and anti-aircraft fire are suppressed. Unfortunately, neither of these contingencies can be relied upon by the withdrawing force. Strategic-lift aircraft and civilian airliners are vulnerable even to small-arms fire. Even if a landing strip can be held, indirect artillery and mortar fire can make the landing of fixed-wing aircraft extremely dangerous. The widespread proliferation of man-portable surface-to-air missiles further increases the vulnerability of aircraft. A single aircraft destroyed or disabled on a runway can close the airport to further operations. The personnel- and cargo-carrying potential of aircraft are still greatly inferior to the potential possessed by most ships. Amphibious shipping can exploit the security and access provided by control of the sea to extricate friendly forces from even the most high-threat environment. The self-defence capability provided by the associated maritime force can protect the evacuation force as well as provide vital military support to personnel ashore. An amphibious task group can poise at sea, waiting for the call to intervene, and it is available in situations where air access

is at risk. Unfortunately, the use of ships and craft limits the area of withdrawal to the shoreline, although the employment of helicopters extends the reach of an amphibious force many miles inland. Conventional amphibious craft can be used to navigate rivers, estuaries and inland waterways.

PLANNING

In many ways the planning and conduct of an amphibious withdrawal is similar to that for an assault, except that it is conducted in reverse. Rather than building up combat power on the shore until it is high enough to survive without direct support from the sea, combat power is progressively reduced until a stage when the landing force becomes more and more dependent on seaborne support. The organization of forces, responsibility for tasks and command relationships generally remain the same as for an assault, although of course the extemporized nature of many withdrawals may lead to a certain amount of improvisation in the arrangements for command and control and for the provision of shipping and other supporting assets.

Although the planning process is basically the same as that conducted for an assault, amphibious withdrawals have many features which distinguish them from the former type of operation. Pressure of time means that planning processes are usually abridged; indeed, enemy action can mean that the withdrawal is conducted very rapidly. There is unlikely to be time for extensive training, preparations or rehearsals, as there may be for an assault. Unless an undamaged port can be secured, the facilities for embarkation and loading are also likely to be restricted. This can cause numerous logistical problems, particularly for the embarkation of heavy stores, vehicles and equipment. In such circumstances a specialist amphibious force, which is able to land directly on the beach and embark all forms of military and civilian equipment, is a vital asset. Without such ships and craft, the conduct of an amphibious withdrawal can be seriously compromised.

Amphibious withdrawals suffer the same planning limitations as amphibious assaults, with criteria such as terrain, hydrographic conditions and weather playing an important part. An assaulting force has the luxury of choosing the time and place for a landing, maximizing conditions for their own benefit. A defeated land force seeking re-embarkation may not be able to do this. As such, amphibious withdrawals may have to be conducted in places where beach conditions, tides and offshore currents are far from ideal. They may have to be conducted in poor weather, and this can place a serious constraint on both beach landings and on helicopter operations. Unlike assaults, withdrawals can rarely ever be postponed to wait for better weather. Enemy activity may force the withdrawal to be conducted under the cover of darkness at night, and this too can add to confusion and dislocation, both on the beach and offshore. The need for effective command and control and for organized beach parties is paramount at this juncture.

The embarkation area must be secured against further enemy activity. This may be particularly difficult when the enemy land forces are in contact with the friendly forces. In such circumstances, a perimeter is held against enemy attack. The bridgehead is progressively reduced through a series of concentric phase-lines as personnel are re-embarked. It is inevitably very difficult to re-embark the final rearguard if the enemy is alert and prepared to attack the withdrawing force.

In such circumstances, and if possible, massive naval fire support and air cover is employed in order to support the withdrawing troops and in order to hinder or deter a final enemy attack.

In general, an amphibious withdrawal is conducted in line with the following sequence. First, while naval, air and land forces protect the bridgehead, non-essential personnel, vehicles and supplies are embarked. Second, combat strength ashore is progressively reduced, leaving the minimum possible covering force to protect the embarkation point. Finally, the covering force is re-embarked. It is at this stage that priority is most often given to personnel rather than equipment. If possible, vehicles, equipment and stores that cannot be embarked will be destroyed. The conduct of a number of actual amphibious withdrawals will be examined in the case studies described later in this chapter.

BELOW: A US Army Stinger. Weapons like this, with a fire-and-forget targeting system and a range of up to 5 miles (8km), can make airlifts exceedingly risky.

NON-COMBATANT EVACUATION OPERATIONS

Non-combatant Evacuation Operations (NEOs) is the name given to operations which involve the withdrawal to safety of entitled civilian non-combatants from locations in foreign countries where they face the threat of hostile action. They are usually conducted in situations where civil control has broken down and local police forces are either unable – or unwilling – to protect civilian lives. They may occur either with or without the support of the host nation, although most commanders prefer to base their planning on a worst-case basis in order to be ready for any contingencies that may arise. NEOs are frequently conducted in situations short of war where political factors remain important. In such cases, the amphibious commander liaises closely with the diplomatic staff in theatre and

may be forced to subjugate military imperatives to political logic. In particular, rules of engagement will be much more constrained in an NEO than they are in conventional military operations. For example, a commander may have to defend the evacuation point without having the authority to pre-empt hostile acts and take any form of preventative military action.

The principles of an NEO have been likened to those of a raid. The landing force establishes forward elements ashore to liaise with the authorities in theatre and to assist them with their own plan for the evacuation. If the situation ashore is hostile, or is potentially hostile, pre-landing forces may be required to secure the embarkation points. Evacuation assembly points are then nominated to act as rendezvous sites for entitled civilian personnel before they are moved to an

BELOW: Stanleyville (now Kisangani), the Congo, 24 November 1964. Under the protection of Belgian Paratroops, freed hostages walk to a transport aircraft to be flown to safety in Leopoldville (Kinshasa). Located far inland, Stanleyville was beyond the range of amphibious forces, necessitating the use of airborne troops in the rescue.

embarkation holding area. At the embarkation holding area, they will be provided with medical assistance – if they need it – and their status as entitled personnel will be checked. Once this has been done, the civilians may then be evacuated, by helicopter, by landing craft or, if possible and if suitable facilities are available, by commercial, rather than military, vessels or aircraft. Throughout the operation, the commander will keep a military force in reserve that will be ready to react to any kind of unforeseen circumstances.

NEOs have been conducted in a variety of different circumstances throughout the 20th century. As the Soviet Army advanced into Eastern Europe in 1944 and 1945, the battered remnants of the German Navy evacuated isolated military and civilian personnel to relative safety in the west. Sources vary, but some estimate that up to two million people were evacuated in this way. More recently, in January 1986 the British Royal Yacht, supported by two warships and a fleet auxiliary, evacuated 1379 men, women and children of 55 nationalities from Aden. This was during a time of civil unrest and most of those evacuated were brought out from open beaches by the Royal Yacht's own boats. NEOs have been a frequent occurrence in the unstable conditions that have existed since the end of the Cold War. United States Amphibious Ready Groups and their embarked Marines have conducted numerous evacuations, and in the process have safeguarded thousands of lives. Examples of these include Operation Sharp Edge, when 1600 civilians were evacuated from Monrovia (Liberia) in 1990; Operation United Shield, where 23 ships and 16,000 Marines safeguarded the withdrawal of UN forces from Mogadishu (Somalia) in 1995; Operation Silver Wake which involved the evacuation of civilians from Albania in 1997 after the breakdown of order in that country; and Operation Safe Departure in 1998 when 172 civilians were withdrawn from Eritrea due to the threat of conflict over a border dispute with their neighbours in Ethiopia.

NEOs have not been a purely American activity; European forces have also been active in this area of operations. In 1998 the French 3rd Parachutiste Infanterie Marine and No. 40 Commando of the British Royal Marines participated in a joint mission to Brazzavile in the Congo from which point they were ready to

ABOVE: USN SEAL, Monrovia, Liberia, April 1996 during Operation Sharp Edge. US amphibious capabilities were again deployed to evacuate civilians in Liberia in 1996, during operation Assured Response. The ships involved in Assured Response included the helicopter carrier (LPH) USS *Guam*, the landing platform dock (LPD) USS *Trenton*, and the landing ship dock (LSD) USS *Portland*.

RIGHT: A US Marine at Mogadishu airport, Somalia, during Operation Restore Hope, December 1992. Although begun as a humanitarian operation to protect the distribution of food, UN forces became sucked into a vicious conflict with the faction led by Mohammad Aideed. Amphibious forces provided the necessary bulk evacuation capability.

conduct an NEO from Kinshasa across the Congo River in neighbouring Zaire. Although they arrived by air, the Marines were equipped with amphibious craft to enable them to conduct a withdrawal across the river. As conflict and instability remain a constant feature in world affairs, it appears likely that NEOs will remain an important military task in the future.

CASE STUDY: GALLIPOLI, 1915–16

The Gallipoli landings are very well documented in many histories of World War I. The failure of the Allied expedition to achieve its objectives left two shallow bridgeheads on the Gallipoli peninsula. A series of costly attacks and counter-attacks saw the Allies fail to break out of their lodgements and the Turks fail to push them into the sea. However, the stalemate could not last forever. By the autumn of 1915, the approaching winter promised to make conditions at Gallipoli

extremely unpleasant and rough seas would inevitably make the supply and reinforcement of the lodgements difficult. In addition to this, many believed that the troops which were tied up at Gallipoli could be more usefully employed elsewhere. In October 1915 General Sir Charles Monro was appointed as Commander in Chief of the Mediterranean Expeditionary Force and, after inspecting his new command, he recommended the evacuation of the Dardanelles Army. This move was approved by the British Cabinet on 7 December of that year.

The process of withdrawal was fraught with danger. The northern lodgement at Suvla Bay – ANZAC Cove – included 83,000 men, 5000 animals and 200 artillery pieces. The southern lodgement at Cape Helles 13 miles (21km) away had roughly half the number of men and both areas were under the direct observation of the Turkish Army. The plan for the evacuation had three stages. The first, called the Preliminary Stage, involved the evacuation of all men, equipment and animals that were not required to defend the lodgement; this stage began even prior to the official order to withdraw. During the second stage, called the Intermediate Stage, the remaining garrison would be reduced over a period of 10 days to the minimum capacity required to hold a Turkish attack for one week. This was thought necessary as bad weather might delay the embarkation of the rearguard for this time. The third stage, called the Final Stage, would involve the withdrawal of the rearguard at the first opportunity. Monro expected this stage to take no more than two nights, and priority was to be placed on saving men rather than equipment. Surprise was essential; some trenches at the Suvla Bay lodgement were only 10yds (9m) from the Turkish lines. If the Turks realized that a withdrawal was under way, they could counter-attack, possibly overwhelming the rearguard and inflicting heavy casualties.

The original plan was to evacuate forces from Suvla Bay, but not from Cape Helles. The decision to withdraw all forces from Gallipoli had not yet been taken and, in any case, there were insufficient boats to evacuate all of the forces at once. Two alternative plans were developed. One plan, which employed the conventional approach of gradually reducing forces within a shrinking perimeter, had the disadvantage of signalling to the Turks that a withdrawal was under way. However, secrecy was all important and so an alternative plan was adopted. It was decided to hold the existing lines, but to progressively reduce numbers, maintaining an outward show of normality and giving the Turks no reason to believe that a withdrawal was actually happening. Thus, while troops and equipment were re-embarked at night, their tents were left standing, empty supply boxes were delivered and stacked on the beach, and fires and cooking stoves were lit in empty dugouts. Troops that remained in the bridgehead created as much noise and activity as possible to hide the fact that their numbers were drastically reducing. To prepare for this, as early as 23 November

the commanders had started 'quiet periods' where there would be no offensive activity. In this way, the Turks became accustomed to periods of relative inactivity within the Allied lines.

The withdrawal progressed smoothly. By the completion of the Intermediate Stage, the force which was stationed ashore had been reduced in numbers from 83,000 men to only 20,000 men. These remaining troops were then withdrawn over two nights on 18 and 19 December. The most dangerous point occurred on 19 December when the final rearguard of 10,000 men was in the process of embarking. This was the stage at which the army was most vulnerable, as troops left defensive positions on the front line and gathered on the beach for embarkation. In order to cover this retreat, numerous mines and booby-traps were laid, and troops placed barbed-wire barriers behind them to block the trenches as they left. In order to give the impression that the trenches were still manned, rifles were fixed with a variety of ingenious devices so that they would fire at random times even after the last troops had left. Remarkably, this evacuation was a complete success. The last boats left the lodgement at 0500 hours in the morning, torching huge piles

ABOVE: Trenches on the crest of Lone Pine, a hill in the ANZAC sector of the Gallipoli front. Lone Pine was evacuated at around 0315 on 21 December 1915. The withdrawal went unnoticed by the enemy, despite the fact that Turkish positions were only a dozen or so yards away.

of surplus equipment before they set off. The Turks did not realize what had happened until it was too late to intervene. A total of 83,000 men, 186 guns and 4695 horses and mules had been withdrawn at a total cost of only two men wounded at Suvla Bay and nine artillery pieces abandoned and destroyed. Remarkably, not a single man was left behind at Gallipoli.

However, the withdrawal of troops in the north had obvious implications for the lodgement at Cape Helles. It meant that the Turks would now be able to concentrate their entire force against the remaining lodgement. As a result, on 27 December the British Cabinet decided to withdraw the remaining forces from Helles, a total of 35,000 men. This withdrawal would be even more difficult than that undertaken from Suvla Bay, as the Turks were now aware of the possibility of a secret evacuation. In addition to this, while at Suvla the front line had been as little as 1500yds (1372m) from the sea, at Helles it was around 4 miles (6.4km) away, leaving the rearguard a considerable distance from the safety of

BELOW: Admiral Sir Bertram Home Ramsey, KCG, MVO in 1943. In 1940, the then Vice Admiral Ramsey commanded Operation Dynamo, the Dunkirk withdrawal. The Dunkirk operation prevented a military defeat from becoming a total disaster.

their boats. Nevertheless, preparations got under way, and were similar to those at Suvla. In addition, French forces at Helles were withdrawn and replaced by British troops from the 29th Division in order to simplify command arrangements. By 7 January 1916 the garrison was reduced to only 19,000 men. It was at this point that the Turkish forces launched a major offensive, preceded by the largest artillery bombardment of the campaign. However, the depleted garrison beat off the offensive, repulsing the attack with such vigour that the Turkish Army and their German advisers were convinced that no evacuation was planned. The final embarkation occurred on 6 January, when the rearguard of 17,000 men was embarked in one night, without loss. The final boat sailed at 0400 hours, four hours after the last man had left the front line.

The two withdrawals from Gallipoli were meticulously planned and expertly conducted. They are outstanding examples of the successful employment of amphibious seapower, and stand in stark contrast to the original assault of April 1915. To withdraw a military force which is in direct contact with the enemy from observed beaches, within range of enemy artillery, virtually without casualty and with the vast majority of their artillery and equipment intact was indeed a remarkable achievement. The Allies were fortunate that the Royal Navy had undisputed command of the seas off the south and west coasts of Gallipoli and that the weather remained reasonably clear during both operations. The night after the evacuation from Suvla Bay, bad weather brought heavy seas that washed away the makeshift embarkation piers. Likewise, deteriorating weather during the withdrawal from Helles had complicated the final embarkation. Most importantly, various measures were employed successfully to deceive the enemy, and these forestalled a potential offensive and enabled the rearguard to withdraw without loss.

CASE STUDY: DUNKIRK, 1940

The withdrawal of the British Expeditionary Force (BEF) from Dunkirk in June 1940 was one of the key events of World War II. Over 338,000 British and Allied troops were saved from capture and taken to safety. The fact that the BEF was saved had an important effect on British morale and provided vital troops for the defence of the British Isles against any German airborne or amphibious invasion. Success came at a price, however, as the withdrawal was strongly opposed by the Germans. In particular, the experience at Dunkirk clearly demonstrated the difficulty inherent in conducting withdrawals at short notice, with neither harbour facilities nor air superiority.

In May 1940 German armoured forces smashed through Allied defences in France and Belgium, isolating large numbers of Allied troops. On 22 May, the German Army Group B, exploiting behind British and French lines, reached the Channel coast near Abbeville and managed to isolate the Allied Northern Army Group, including the BEF. The Germans then swung north, moving against the Channel ports and threatening to cut off the Northern Army Group from the coast. As early as 19 May the British had begun to investigate the possibility of evacuating isolated military forces from the Channel coast. As the situation in France deteriorated, it became clear that a larger operation would now be necessary. Facing overwhelming odds, the BEF conducted a fighting retreat to Dunkirk, a small port close to the Belgian border. By 26 May, the BEF had secured a perimeter around Dunkirk itself, and by 29 May they had been joined by the French 1st Army. The creation of the perimeter was helped by stubborn defences at Calais and Boulogne that delayed the German advance, as well as by Hitler's inexplicable decision on 24 May to temporarily halt the advance of his Panzers.

On 26 May Vice-Admiral Ramsey, Flag Officer Commanding Dover, received the signal that Operation Dynamo – as the evacuation from Dunkirk was code-named – would begin. Between 26 May and 4 June, when the operation was completed, a total of 222 naval vessels and 665 merchant craft successfully embarked 338,226 men. They achieved this despite the constant air attack by the Luftwaffe, which inflicted heavy losses in shipping and destroyed the port facilities in the town. The maritime force employed for the operation at Dunkirk was international in nature. The Royal Navy's contribution included 39 destroyers, one cruiser, six corvettes and 38 minesweepers. These were supplemented by 36 passenger ferries, seven hospital ships and numerous stores ships, tugs, drifters and fishing vessels. The French Navy contributed 19 destroyers and torpedo boats and ships and craft were provided by the French, Dutch and Belgian merchant navies.

RAF fighters flown in from Britain were able to provide a measure of air cover over Dunkirk but they could not stop the German forces from sinking six destroyers and nine personnel ships, nor from causing serious damage to many

LEFT: The French destroyer *Bourrasque* sinking at Dunkirk. Without air superiority, amphibious withdrawals can be a costly and dangerous business. Six destroyers were lost as well as many other vessels during the evacuation. The Allies were fortunate that the German Navy was too weak to intervene.

ABOVE: The port facilities at Dunkirk were destroyed by German air attacks. This, combined with a lack of specialist amphibious equipment, slowed down the rate at which troops could be evacuated. Despite the risks involved it was therefore decided to moor ships alongside the damaged harbour mole and most troops were evacuated in this manner.

more. German aircraft also attacked troops waiting to be evacuated from the beach, although here the soft sand reduced the effect of aerial bombing. In spite of the damage inflicted by the Luftwaffe, bombing alone proved to be unable to halt the withdrawal. The Allies were fortunate that the German Navy did not play a part in the operation. Heavy losses during the invasion of Norway had exacerbated the Kriegsmarine's inferiority to the British and French Navies, and it was therefore unable to hinder the process of withdrawal. The German Army pressed hard against the perimeter of the lodgement, but was held off to the last by the tenacious defence of the rearguard.

At the outset of the operation there

were two routes into Dunkirk from England. Route Z ran directly from Dover to Calais and then eastward along the coast to Dunkirk. At only 39 miles (63km) long, this would have been both the shortest and the quickest route. However, as early as 27 May, the German advance placed Route Z within range of land-based artillery, making it too dangerous to use. An alternative, Route Y, was employed, and this required vessels to sail north of the Goodwin Sands off Kent and then due east, beyond Dunkirk, before turning to sail south-west to the site of the withdrawal. This route was more secure, but at 87 miles (140km) long, it was twice the length of Route Z, which doubled the transit time and consequently halved the potential troop lift. Later in the operation, Ramsey initiated a new route, Route X. This ran between the other routes and at only 55 miles (88km) long it was a considerable improvement on Route Y. In fact, it took the Germans three days to realize that this new route was being taken.

The destruction of the port facilities at Dunkirk made embarkation difficult and the coastline around Dunkirk was not particularly suitable for an amphibious withdrawal. A mixture of gently shelving sandy beaches and offshore shoals meant that only small craft could get in close enough to the shore to embark troops. Even then, the men had to wade out a long way under the constant threat of air attack. At this stage in the war, Britain did not have a significant amphibious capability and so specialist landing ships and craft were not available. The Admiralty initially believed that the withdrawal could last only two nights and that a maximum of number of around 44,000 troops would be saved. On the first night of Dynamo, only 7669 men were evacuated; this must have seemed an extremely low figure to the Admiralty. Consequently, the next day it was decided to berth ships directly against the damaged mole outside the harbour. In this way, men could be embarked direct into large ships without having to transfer from small boats. This proved to be a success and 17,804 men and some equipment was evacuated on 28 May. At the same time, the British Government called upon the seafaring people of southern Britain to join the struggle. Civilian small craft, fishing vessels, sailing yachts, tugs and pleasure craft sailed to Dunkirk to participate in the withdrawal. Although the majority of troops were evacuated by large naval and merchant ships from the mole, these small craft nevertheless played a vital supplementary role and took off many additional troops from the shallow beach. In stark contrast to the first night of Operation Dynamo, on 31 May 68,104 Allied troops were embarked in that single day.

By 1 June the severity of enemy air activity forced the remaining evacuation to be conducted at night. By this stage, the naval crews were approaching exhaustion after many days and nights of ceaseless activity. The British rearguard embarked on 2 June, leaving French forces to man the perimeter. By 4 June, a combination of naval losses, enemy air activity and pressure from German land forces meant that the operation was effectively ended. It was impossible to embark the final rearguard, due to the proximity and vigilance of enemy ground forces, but their sacrifice enabled the BEF and over 110,000 French troops to be saved, at a cost of 40,000 men captured. Around 71 heavy guns and 600 vehicles were also evacuated from Dunkirk. However, the BEF was forced to abandon the vast majority of its tanks, guns and heavy equipment in France, as a consequence leaving Britain dangerously short of these weapons in the following months. If the withdrawal had been

ABOVE: The Dunkirk evacuation. This picture amply demonstrates the vulnerability of the withdrawing troops as they struggle to reach the awaiting transports. The difficulty of embarking without port facilities is readily apparent.

ABOVE: Marines of the 1st US Marine Division during the fight to reach Hungnam. From November to December 1950, the Marines fought their way back through Hagaru-ri, down mountain trails back to the sea taking with them their equipment and wounded. Also involved in this 'advance to the sea' was 41 (Independent) Commando, Royal Marines.

supported by specialist amphibious ships, able to beach and then embark the heaviest of army equipment, there is little doubt that more of this equipment could have been saved. The presence of specialist amphibious ships would also have made the embarkation process quicker and less dangerous.

In the days after Dunkirk, there were many more amphibious withdrawals from France. They were conducted from a variety of ports including Cherbourg, St Malo, Brest and St Nazaire. Although generally less hazardous than the evacuation from Dunkirk, these operations were not conducted without loss. For example, at St Nazaire, 3000 lives were lost when the liner *Lancastria* was sunk by air attack as it left the harbour. Over 190,000 troops were saved by these latter withdrawals; the majority were

British but they included 18,000 French, 24,000 Polish and 5000 Czech troops. Almost exactly one year later the Royal Navy conducted two further withdrawals saving defeated Allied forces from Greece (April 1941) and Crete (May–June 1941), once again denying the Germans the full fruits of their victories.

CASE STUDY: KOREA, 1950

The Korean War is more usually remembered for the brilliant amphibious assault at Inchon in September 1950. However, the ability to withdraw troops using amphibious shipping was also to prove important. An early example of this occurred on 16 August 1950 when the 3rd South Korean Division was surrounded by enemy forces near Yonghae on the east coast. Four LSTs supported by the cruiser USS *Helena* and some destroyers evacuated a total of 5830 military personnel, 1260 civilians and over 100 vehicles without loss of personnel or equipment. The next day the division was landed behind friendly lines and was immediately back in action. Without this means of escape, the division may have been lost.

More famous was the evacuation of X Corps from the port of Hungnam in December 1950. By this stage, the Korean War had undergone a dramatic reverse. In his successful drive through North Korea, General MacArthur ignored increasingly urgent warnings about the potential of Chinese intervention. The Chinese were keen to support their Communist ally and were increasingly concerned by what appeared to be a UN advance right up to their border at the Yalu river. Consequently, on 27 November Chinese forces infiltrated across the border and launched a massive and enormously successful assault on X Corps and 8th Army. MacArthur had allowed these units to become separated and strung out and thus they became easy prey to the concentrated Chinese forces. The 8th Army was able to conduct a retreat back into South Korean territory but X Corps was not so lucky as it was badly dispersed and faced 12 Chinese divisions. In a series of desperate encounters, the outlying force of 1st US Marine Division, reinforced by 41 Independent Commando, Royal Marines was able to extricate itself from a dangerous position inland at the Chosin Reservoir and 'advanced to the sea' back to the port of Hungnam, where it was joined by the remainder of X Corps, the 3rd and 7th Infantry Divisions. Facing overwhelming odds, the Corps found itself in a position akin to the BEF in 1940, needing to re-embark to safety while remaining in contact with a superior enemy force.

They sought to achieve this with a phased withdrawal, utilizing a system of phase lines whereby the beachhead would get progressively smaller until all forces were withdrawn. In this they were supported by a massive concentration of naval gunfire and by carrier aviation which ruled the skies over the city. Remarkably the operation was a resounding success. This was helped by the fact that the port facilities at Hungnam remained intact; the United States destroyed them once the withdrawal was complete.

The first wave of US Marines reached Hungnam on 10 December and began

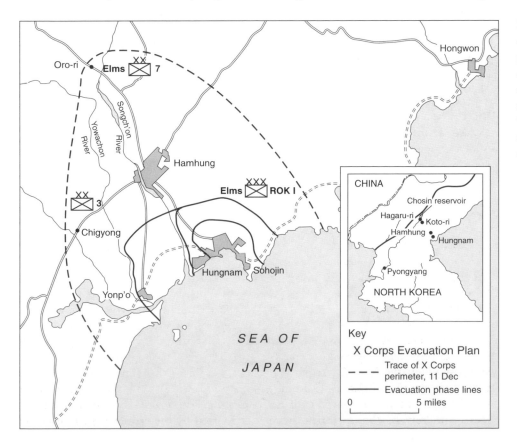

LEFT: The Hungnam withdrawal. A well-organized, phased contraction of the defensive perimeter allowed nearly 200,000 troops and refugees to be evacuated. The operation was greatly facilitated by UN dominance of the sea and air.

RIGHT: Drums of aviation gasoline at Hungnam, ready to be loaded onto an LST, 14 December 1950. With the harbour facilities undamaged and a ready supply of amphibious shipping, the Hungnam evacuation was able to take off large quantities of both stores and equipment.

BELOW: Hungnam harbour, December 1950. The high-speed transport USS *Begor* lies at anchor ready to load the last UN landing craft as a huge explosion rips apart the harbour installations. The UN forces demolished the harbour facilities as they left.

embarkation, completing four days later. They were followed by South Korean troops and then 7th and 3rd Divisions. The final embarkation occurred on Christmas Eve 1950 and was covered by what was described as 'a curtain of steel laid down by the navy'.

The Chinese made a number of attempts to assault the perimeter. However, by 24 December they had learnt the devastating effect of concentrated naval gunfire and did not seriously disrupt proceedings. A total of 105,000 troops and 91,000 civilian refugees were taken off. In stark contrast to British evacuations at Dunkirk and Crete, they also came off with their equipment, taking 17,500 vehicles and 350,000 tonnes of stores. This was enormously significant. Unlike the BEF

LEFT: Carrier-based aircraft made a critical contribution to the success of the evacuation. Combined with extensive NGS, air attack helped to even the odds on the defensive perimeter, compensating for the gradual withdrawal of ground forces to the ships.

in 1940, X Corps remained a properly equipped fighting formation ready to return to the front line at short notice. This is in fact precisely what happened, and the troops and equipment saved at Hungnam played a vital role in stabilizing the UN lines south of the 38th parallel. In fact, it is hard to see how the UN could have halted the Chinese offensive without X Corps. As such, the withdrawal from Hungnam should stand alongside Inchon as one of the decisive events of the Korean War.

CONCLUSION

In the aftermath of the withdrawal from Dunkirk, Winston Churchill famously noted that wars are not won by evacuations. This is obviously true and evacuations are inevitably associated with defeat rather than victory. However, the ability to save personnel and matériel from capture or destruction can prove vital in allowing a defeated army to recover. The existence of a balanced amphibious force can often considerably ease the problems of re-embarkation, particularly when conventional harbour facilities are not available. Without specialist amphibious ships, it may not be possible to save vehicles, artillery or other heavy equipment and even the embarkation of personnel may prove to be slow and difficult.

The inclusion of helicopter assets in an amphibious force allows withdrawals to be conducted at some distance from the shore; this can be of particular value in non-combatant evacuations, where the requirement to lift heavy military stores is absent. The large number of NEOs in recent years suggests that the need to conduct amphibious withdrawals in the future will remain.

CHAPTER EIGHT

AMPHIBIOUS EQUIPMENT

Amphibious operations require specialist equipment in order to overcome the challenges posed by natural hazards and enemy action.

In order to be carried out successfully, amphibious operations usually need a wide variety of specialist amphibious ships, craft and equipment. They also need a broad range of supporting assets, including naval and airforce units which are designed to ensure the safe arrival of the task force in theatre and to secure and exploit control of the littoral battlespace. Although there are exceptions to this rule – as when the Soviet Union conducted a number of successful operations during World War II, despite a paucity of specialist shipping – the ability to land large, balanced forces after a long sea crossing and against enemy action usually requires a broad range of specialist equipment. In the early years of the 20th century this fact was frequently ignored, but the experiences of World War I highlighted it, and the lesson was reinforced by a series of operations in both the European and Pacific theatres during World War II. Today, many navies maintain dedicated amphibious forces, which range in size and capability from that of Nigeria, which operates one old LST, to the United States, which has 12 Amphibious Ready Groups, each with a greater lift potential than most other navies possess.

LEFT: The LHD USS *Wasp* transits the Surnadal fjord in Norway on 9 March 1995, during the NATO Exercise Strong Resolve. At 40,000 tonnes, and capable of embarking 1870 troops, 12 landing craft and 32 CH-46E Sea Knight helicopters, the *Wasp*-class ships are probably the most capable amphibious vessels afloat.

ABOVE: US Marines practise unloading artillery from a prototype landing craft between the wars. The US Navy experimented with a variety of different vessels but did not find a suitable landing craft until they adapted the Higgins boat for military service in the late 1930s.

Prior to World War I, landing craft had developed little from the flat-bottomed rowing boats which were used during the age of sail. In the absence of more appropriate craft, troops assaulted the beach in a variety of rowing boats and dumb lighters. The only advantage which technology brought was the use of steam launches which were able to pull strings of these craft close inshore; the oarsmen would then complete the journey. Landing the necessary artillery, horses and vehicles was a difficult and usually laborious process. The clear inadequacy of such methods led the British to use a converted collier, the *River Clyde*, during their initial landings at Gallipoli. At the Suvla Bay landings in August 1915, some specialist landing craft (X Craft) were employed. During the inter-war period, the Americans and the British independently studied the need for specialist landing craft and, as a result of their studies, built prototype vessels. The Japanese in particular made significant progress and developed a number of ships and craft that they employed to good effect during their war with China. Notable amongst these was the Shinshu Maru, a 8000-tonne ship which had the ability to launch assault craft from a stern ramp or load troops onto landing craft through doors on the ship's sides. British and American observers noted the performance of Japanese landing ships off Shanghai in 1937 and were spurred on to make further developments of their own.

The need to conduct a series of opposed landings during World War II forced the UK and the USA to develop their limited amphibious capabilities until, by 1945, both nations possessed an unprecedented range and scale of specialist equipment. For example, by the end of the war the British alone possessed over 5000 ships, craft and landing barges of all varieties, and over 100 amphibious vehicles. The US inventory was even more extensive. Landing ships and craft were designed to undertake all kinds of roles, from the 4000-tonne sea-going LST, which was able to carry 20 tanks and numerous trucks on an ocean voyage and land them through its bow doors within wading depth, to the ubiquitous LCVP, which was capable of carrying 36 men from their mother ship to the shore. Ships and craft were designed to carry infantry, vehicles, artillery and stores. Other vessels were built or adapted to operate as headquarters ships, air-defence control ships and navigation control craft, while still more were adapted to carry and administer the hundreds of minor landing craft which were needed to bring the assault troops to shore, but which lacked the range and speed to sail independently to the assault area. A list of the different types of landing ships and craft is given in Appendix One.

In the past, warships and merchant vessels have frequently been used to transport the amphibious force. Warships in particular have the advantage that they tend to be fast and are usually equipped with an impressive array of offensive and defensive weaponry. Also, due to a warship's conventional appearance, if it is detected by the enemy, they will not necessarily realize an amphibious landing is about to take place. Unfortunately, although many frigates, destroyers and cruisers can provide some temporary accommodation for a number of troops, they lack the facilities to support a large, embarked force; they are also unable to accommodate large vehicles or heavy stockpiles of supplies and ammunition. Most importantly, conventional warships are not designed to carry large numbers of landing craft or troop-carrying helicopters. Although a small number of assault craft can be embarked, and most warships have a small helicopter flight deck, reliance on such facilities can

BELOW: US troops land from a LST during World War II. The LST was designed to be run aground on the beach, before the bow doors opened and troops and vehicles could land on the shore or in shallow water using the ship's ramp. While useful for such landings, the shallow draught and bow doors of the LST reduced overall speed and also seaworthiness.

BELOW: British Landing Craft Assault (LCA) during World War II. The LCA differed from its American counterpart, the Higgins boat, in that it was lightly armoured and had a measure of overhead protection for the embarked troops. Both types of landing craft were produced in huge numbers throughout the war.

seriously restrict the initial troop lift and greatly complicate reinforcement and supply arrangements.

Larger warships such as aircraft carriers have a greater potential as makeshift amphibious ships. The small British *Invincible*-class aircraft carriers have a secondary role as helicopter assault ships. In what is known as the 'fast dash' role, the carrier's large flight deck and hangar enables it to carry a commando unit, as well as the helicopters required to land them. In actuality, the earliest helicopter assault ships were converted aircraft carriers. However, unless specifically modified for this role, aircraft carriers are not as effective as purpose-built ships and using a carrier in this way stops it from fulfilling its primary mission, which is to conduct fixed-wing air operations. History has proved conclusively that, except in certain small-scale operations, there is no substitute for specialist amphibious shipping.

LANDING CRAFT

Most modern landing craft owe their origins to the World War II-era Landing Craft Vehicle, Personnel (LCVP), which was adapted from a craft designed in the

1920s by the New Orleans boat-builder, Andrew J. Higgins. The 'Higgins boat' had a shallow draft which allowed it to beach in shallow water and it could carry between 30 and 36 troops with a top speed of 8 knots. It had neither the range nor the sea-keeping qualities to conduct a long ocean passage, but was light enough to be carried at ships' davits and then lowered to the sea once the mother ship had reached an inshore position. Later versions borrowed a design feature from the British Landing Craft, Assault (LCA), incorporating a bow ramp to facilitate the discharge of troops or a light vehicle such as a jeep.

Modern LCVPs tend to be larger than their wartime predecessor and many of them have increased speed and range. For example, the Dutch LCVP Mk III is bigger and heavier than the Higgins boat and, at 14 knots loaded, is considerably faster. However, it carries a similar military load and performs the same function as the earlier vessel. The new British LCVP Mk 5 can achieve 25 knots and has a range of 210 miles (338km) but is still in essence a more advanced version of a craft used over 50 years ago. Capabilities have increased but design principles remain the same. This is true of larger landing craft designed to carry heavy vehicles such as the Landing Craft, Utility (LCU). A key feature common to both the LCU and the LCVP is the requirement for them to be carried into theatre in a mother ship. As more modern craft gain increased range and speed, this requirement may diminish but it is unlikely to be removed completely. By their very nature, shallow-draft landing craft with bow doors are relatively unseaworthy and they lack the range of capabilities offered by larger, more capable vessels.

Many navies and marine corps use specialist raiding craft. These can either be inflatable or rigid-hulled, and are sometimes a combination of both. Methods of propulsion vary from inboard and outboard motors to simple hand paddles. The latter are particularly valuable when stealth is at a premium and also when a long journey to shore is not required. A typical inflatable boat with an outboard motor can carry eight troops at speeds of around 20 knots. Rigid craft are more suitable for long journeys or when

speed is at a premium but they are less easy to stow than fully inflatable craft.

AMPHIBIOUS SHIPS

Ships built after 1945 often bear a resemblance to their wartime ancestors. This is inevitable as they have been designed to conduct the same roles and operate under the same limitations. Landing ships must combine lift capacity with survivability, endurance, speed and appropriate command and communications facilities. They must also be able to land their cargo on a hostile shore without relying on conventional port facilities. This may be achieved through landing craft carried on davits or transported in a floodable dock or by helicopters operating from the ship's flight deck. If troops are to be embarked for an extended period, then standards of habitability need to be high and there has to be enough space for the embarked force to keep fit and practise basic drills.

Some large ships, such as the LST, are designed to land their loads directly onto the beach. If this is the case, then they have a shallow draft in order to discharge the vehicles within wading distance. Ships and craft designed to land vehicles will require either a bow ramp or bow doors that open up so that vehicles can exit. This may be combined with a stern ramp and a through deck which allows roll-on, roll-off procedures. Shallow draft and bow doors or ramps undermine the seaworthiness of a vessel and lead to reduced speed, and so some ships use innovative design features to overcome these problems. In the US *Newport*-class LSTs, the bow doors open above the waterline, and vehicles disembark over a

BELOW: The LST USS *Fairfax County* (foreground) sails in company with the LPH USS *Inchon. Newport*-class LSTs such as the *Fairfax County* employ a ramp that is lowered to the beach from the long arms protruding from the ship's bows. This allows the bow doors to open above the waterline which gives the ships greater speed than traditional LSTs.

One way of avoiding the design limitations of the LST is to launch troops and vehicles from LCUs and LCVPs carried in dock-landing ships. Developed from the World War II-era Landing Ship, Dock (LSD), modern LSDs – like the US *Whidbey Island* class – and Landing Platform, Docks (LPD) – such as the Russian *Mitrofan Moskalenko* and the Dutch *Rotterdam* – carry landing craft or air-cushion vehicles in a stern dock. In order to launch the craft, the dock is flooded and the loaded craft can then sail in and out of the stern gate. This allows the larger vessel to remain at some distance from the shore and means that it no longer needs to beach. The drawback of this is that the limited cargo-carrying ability of the LPD's small craft means that it takes longer to land a load than if it were landed directly onto the beach from a LST. However, as large ships are vulnerable to enemy fire and there are a limited number of beaches on which they can operate, the use of small craft from LPDs or similar ships is often the preferred means of landing the initial assault-waves. The introduction of fast, modern landing craft significantly reduces the time taken to land both troops and equipment.

The LST and the LSD/LPD are two of the most important and most commonplace types of amphibious ship. The third is the helicopter assault ship (LPH). The use of helicopters in amphibious operations has been the most

ABOVE: The British LPDs HMS *Fearless* and *Intrepid*. Designed and built during the 1960s these assault ships provided the core of Britain's amphibious fleet throughout the remainder of the 20th century and played a vital role during the Falklands conflict. Both ships are due to be replaced between 2002 and 2003 by the new LPDs HMS *Bulwark* and *Albion*.

RIGHT: Stern view of the Landing Ship Dock (LSD) USS *Anchorage*. In common with other LSDs and LPDs the *Anchorage*-class ships launch landing craft by lowering their stern gate, flooding the internal well deck and floating out loaded landing craft, amphibious vehicles or LCACs.

long ramp extending in front of the ship, supported by long arms that protrude over the bows. In this way, the *Newport*-class ships can sail at a speed of 20 knots, compared to 15 knots for the preceding *Terrebonne Parish* class.

LEFT: The *Iwo Jima*-class LPH
USS *Inchon*. The *Iwo Jima*-
class ships were the first
purpose-built helicopter
carriers and their appearance
helped to revolutionize the
conduct of amphibious
warfare. The USS *Inchon* was
launched in 1969 and in
1996 it was converted to a
Mine Counter-measures
Command, Control and
Support Ship.

radical development in this field since
1945. Using them in this role was
pioneered by the USMC during the late
1940s and 1950s. In 1955 the old escort
carrier, the USS *Thetis Bay*, was
converted into the first LPH. Capable of
carrying 1000 troops and 20 HRS type
helicopters, the *Thetis Bay* represented a
radical departure in the conduct of

amphibious operations. By 1959 the
USA had begun work on new purpose-
built LPHs of the *Iwo Jima* class.
Displacing 18,000 tonnes fully loaded,
the *Iwo Jima* was 592ft (180m) long and
could embark around 2000 troops and
up to 30 medium-lift helicopters. Seven
of these new ships were launched in
the years between 1960 and 1969.

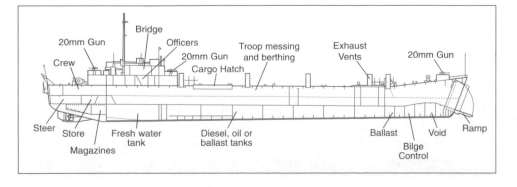

LEFT: A line drawing of the
World War II era LST(2).
The first LSTs were designed
and built in Britain. The
LST(2) was built in the
United States and provided
the backbone of all Allied
landings after its operational
debut in 1943.

RIGHT: The British 'commando carrier' HMS *Bulwark* photographed towards the end of its career in the 1970s. *Bulwark* had started life as a conventional light aircraft carrier and conducted airstrikes against Egypt in 1956. After conversion to a commando carrier she saw extensive service overseas and played a vital part in the deterrence of Iraqi aggression against Kuwait in 1961.

Using helicopters brought a new concept of 'vertical envelopment' to amphibious warfare, whereby troops landed in helicopters could outflank enemy defensive positions on the beach and land at advantageous positions further inland. The first ever amphibious helicopter assault was conducted by No. 45 Commando, Royal Marines flying from the aircraft carriers HMS *Ocean* and HMS *Theseus* during the landings at Port Said in 1956. Following this operation, the British converted two 22,000-tonne aircraft carriers, HMS *Bulwark* in 1960 and *Albion* in 1962 to operate in the LPH role. These ships were known to the British as 'commando carriers'. It is worth noting that, despite being larger and heavier than the purpose-built US *Iwo Jima*-class ships, *Bulwark* and *Albion* carried a much smaller military load of 750 troops; converted ships are rarely as efficient in their new role as a purpose-built vessel. Due to changing defence priorities, the Royal Navy de-commissioned the commando carriers in the 1970s and they were not replaced. Consequently, the British lacked an LPH during the Falklands conflict and this significantly limited their options during the amphibious landing and the land campaign that followed.

A key weakness of the LPH is its relative inability to land any heavy equipment. Even modern heavy-lift helicopters cannot lift tanks or armoured personnel carriers and these vehicles are also too heavy to be embarked in LCVPs. In order to address this weakness, in the 1960s the USA developed the *Tarawa*-class LHA, a ship that combined the large flight deck of the LPH with the added ability to launch conventional landing craft through a stern dock, in a similar fashion to an LPD. In the 1980s the LHA was followed by the *Wasp*-class LHD, which has improved dock facilities. At 40,000 tonnes fully loaded, they are larger than most non-US aircraft carriers and can carry 1870 troops, 12 landing craft or three LCACs. They can operate 32 CH-46E Sea Knight helicopters and, in their secondary role as a sea-control ship, have the capacity to operate 20 AV-8B Harrier jets. The seven *Wasp*-class ships presently owned by the US Navy are currently the most capable amphibious ships afloat.

Few other navies have purpose-built helicopter assault ships. In 1998 the British commissioned a new LPH, HMS *Ocean*. This ship is designed to embark and support a battalion-sized force. It carries four LCVPs on davits and can operate 12 medium-lift helicopters and six Lynx attack helicopters. The French Navy plans to build two new LHDs, and these are expected to be in service by 2006; the Italian Navy has plans to build a new, multi-purpose aviation-capable ship, designed to operate alongside their aircraft carrier *Giuseppe Garibaldi*. Most modern LPDs have a flight deck suitable for small-scale helicopter operations, and other vessels − such as the Australian landing platform amphibious (LPA) − have a similar capability. A number of navies possess aviation-capable ships that could be employed as assault ships in an emergency. In addition, the Brazilian, French, Italian, Russian, Spanish and Thai Navies all possess aircraft carriers of varying sizes and these can operate as makeshift LPHs in the same manner as the British *Invincible*-class carriers.

FIRE SUPPORT

For an opposed landing to succeed without heavy losses, the defending force must be suppressed or destroyed by friendly fire. In World War II, battleships, cruisers and destroyers used their heavy guns to provide naval gunfire support (NGS) for the assaulting troops. NGS was a vital ingredient in any opposed landing; however, it was rarely sufficient as a force on its own. Naval gunfire consistently proved unable to destroy

well-sited defences, particularly if they were constructed from reinforced concrete. As the assaulting infantry approached the shoreline, the fire of ships offshore had to be lifted to avoid hitting friendly forces. The period of time between the arrival of the first troops ashore and the lifting of the barrage usually enabled the defenders to re-group effectively.

Shallow-draft support craft were needed to accompany the assault-wave close inshore and to provide continuous fire support before, during and after the initial landing; this was one of the key lessons drawn from the failed assault on Dieppe in 1942. As a result, the Allies converted a number of craft to fulfil this role. Most notably, surplus tank landing craft were fitted with a range of weapons, including destroyer guns, anti-aircraft weapons and massed batteries of rockets. The USA designed a purpose-built rocket-firing vessel, called the Landing Ship, Medium (Rocket), and these were to see action during the latter stages of the Pacific War and then again during the Vietnam campaign.

Despite the valuable role played by

BELOW: Viewed from USS *West Virginia*, the USS *Idaho* fires its 14in (356mm) guns at nearly point-blank range during the pre-invasion bombardment of Okinawa, 1 April 1945.

support craft during World War II, very few specialist craft were designed or built after 1945. The USA built only one vessel, the USS *Carronade*, and this saw service during the conflict in Vietnam. A number of navies have fire-support weapons fitted to conventional landing ships and craft; this was a notable feature of landing ships built by the Soviet Union. However, in general, in future, fire support will once again be provided by conventional warships and through close air support. Today, none of the world's navies has the range of capabilities which was available to the United States and Britain in 1945. In part, this reflects the fact that few armed forces anticipate conducting heavily opposed landings. It may also reflect the increased range, accuracy and lethality of precision-guided munitions and the potential use of attack helicopters and carrier-based aircraft to neutralize an enemy defence. Nevertheless, the absence of dedicated fire-support platforms may prove a weakness in certain operations. During the Falklands conflict, the British placed light armoured vehicles in the bows of their LCUs in order to compensate for the absence of such craft. Improvisation like this is unlikely to suffice against a determined opponent.

COMMAND AND CONTROL FACILITIES

Amphibious operations require extensive command and control capabilities. The conventional approach taken prior to

World War II was for commanders to place their headquarters on conventional warships and then move ashore once the lodgement was secure. This had numerous disadvantages. Few warships had the range of communications equipment required to adequately control an amphibious operation. Moreover, naval ships have a range of tasks and duties that can take them away from the landing beaches. This occurred during the North African landings in 1942: General George Patton placed his command on board the cruiser USS *Augusta* but before he could transfer his command ashore, the *Augusta* sailed away from the invasion beaches in order to meet a threatened sortie by some French ships. In order to address these problems, dedicated headquarters ships were developed and were employed to good effect for the remainder of the war.

Today there are very few specialist command and control vessels. The two ships of the US *Blue Ridge* class are the only two purpose-built ships. The US Navy has converted two further vessels, the LPDs USS *Coronado* and *La Salle*, to act as command ships, and their LHAs and LHDs have sophisticated command and control facilities. Large command and control suites can be accommodated within major amphibious ships and this has been built into the design of France's new LHDs which will be fitted out as flagships for joint task force operations. However, such capabilities can be expensive and many ships such as HMS

RIGHT: The US command ships USS *Blue Ridge* and USS *Mount Whitney* (seen here) provide integrated command and control facilities for sea, air and land commanders. As such, they find useful service as fleet flagships for the Seventh Fleet which is based in Japan (*Blue Ridge*) and the Second Fleet based in Virginia (*Mount Whitney*).

Ocean have been completed without the full range of facilities. When ships with advanced command and control suites are not available, operations have to be commanded from other naval vessels. This can pose problems if the vessel does not have room to accommodate the amphibious commander, his planning staff and all of their communications equipment as well.

HELICOPTERS

Helicopters add an extra dimension to amphibious operations. They offer the ability to land troops and equipment from the sea without first having to secure a beach. Helicopters have greater speed and range than landing craft, although they also have a reduced payload. Different helicopters have a varied range of capabilities. For carrying heavy loads, there are heavy-lift aircraft, such as the Boeing Chinook or the Sikorsky CH-53E Super Stallion, which can carry 55 marines or 16 tonnes of equipment. Unfortunately, the size of these aircraft can make them difficult to embark in anything other than the largest amphibious ships; the Chinook can land on the British LPH HMS *Ocean*, but is too large to fit on the elevator that provides access to the

ABOVE: A Royal Navy Westland Sea King lands cargo on the deck of an *Invincible*-class aircraft carrier. The three ships of this class can operate as makeshift amphibious ships in the 'fast dash' role. In this role they act as LPHs, temporarily embarking a commando unit as well as additional commando helicopters.

RIGHT: Attack helicopters such as this Bell AH-1 Cobra combine speed and manoeuvrability with a deadly punch. Deployed from amphibious shipping held offshore, they greatly enhance the offensive and defensive capabilities of an amphibious force. US forces first used Cobras in Vietnam in the 1960s and the first Sea Cobra entered service in 1971. The latest variant operated by the USMC is the AH-1W 'Super Cobra'.

hangar. Smaller, medium-lift aircraft which are able to follow the contours of the ground are usually used to carry infantry in the assault. The Westland Sea King can carry 24 fully equipped troops or a variety of equipment in the cab or slung underneath.

Most helicopters can be fitted with machine-guns to provide them with a measure of self-protection. However, their vulnerability to enemy aircraft and to ground-based anti-aircraft fire means that, ideally, they should be supported by friendly air assets. These may include attack helicopters such as the Bell AH-1W Super Cobra currently in service with the USMC. The Super Cobra has one triple 0.75in (20mm) cannon and eight TOW or hellfire missiles and it can carry two AIM-9L Sidewinder missiles for defence against enemy aircraft. An aircraft with this range of capabilities can also provide valuable close air support for ground forces. The British are planning

to deploy their new and extremely capable Apache attack helicopters from their LPH in addition to its more usual home on the land. However, unlike the Cobra, the Apache was not designed for maritime operations and it remains to be seen whether this aircraft will be able to operate from the deck of a ship.

One recent development that may further increase the potential of helicopter-borne forces is the tilt-rotor aircraft. These aircraft have rotor blades that are able to move from the horizontal, as with a helicopter, to the vertical, as with a conventional aircraft. As such they combine the vertical take-off capability of a helicopter with the extended range and high speed of a fixed-wing aircraft. The USMC is currently developing the MV-22 Osprey tilt-rotor aircraft. Inevitably with such an innovative design, problems have been encountered in the development process. However, it is anticipated that the aircraft will have a range of 1200 miles (1930km) and an operational speed of 270 knots. It will carry 24 fully equipped marines or a 10,000lb (4530kg) external load. It is twice as fast and has four times the range of the CH-46E Sea Knight helicopter that it is designed to replace. The USMC have ordered 400 MV-22s and the aircraft is expected to greatly enhance the operational capabilities of US forces.

AMPHIBIOUS VEHICLES

The Soviet Union developed a number of amphibious light tanks in the 1930s, primarily for use in Russia's wide rivers. This emphasis was maintained after the war and is apparent in equipment such as the PT-76B amphibious tank and the BMP1 Armoured Personnel Carrier, both of which are currently in service with the Russian Naval Infantry. However, no other nation has matched the United States for the range, scale and ingenuity of their amphibious vehicles.

Amphibious vehicles are vehicles able to operate on both land and sea. Inevitably this means compromises in both elements, and such vehicles are rarely as proficient in either environment as single-role assets would be. Nevertheless, the ability to carry infantry and equipment directly from the sea to the beach and then beyond has proved to be of enduring utility. An outstanding example of this was the 2.5-tonne amphibious truck known as the DUKW. Developed during World War II, and used by all Allied forces, the DUKW was a six-wheeled truck with a boat hull, propeller and small rudder. Capable of carrying 25 troops or 5000lb (2265kg), it could manage 5 knots at sea or a maximum of 50mph (80kph) on land. The DUKW was an extremely versatile vehicle in all theatres both during the war and after it. Unfortunately, its slow speed, its lack of protection and its size ashore made it of little use in the assault; it was primarily employed as a ship to shore transport for logistic supplies.

In addition to wheeled amphibious vehicles, the United States also employed a tracked vehicle. Known as Landing Vehicle Tracked (LVT), it was developed by the Marines from a vehicle designed for rescue work in the Everglades. The first LVT-1 was produced in 1941, and,

BELOW: An LVTP-7A1 (AAV-7A1) armoured amphibious vehicle crosses the beach. The distant relative of early LVTs used during World War II, the LVTP-7A1 can carry a Marine platoon directly from the shipping offshore to their target inland. It is due to be replaced in US service by the ultra-modern Advanced Amphibious Assault Vehicle.

ABOVE: US LVTs carrying Marines to the beaches at Iwo Jima in February 1945. The advantage of the LVT over conventional landing craft was its ability to cross coral reefs and other offshore obstacles and to land troops at the back of the beach rather than on the shoreline. The LVTs shown here have two .30-calibre machine-guns mounted forward to provide fire support for the assaulting troops.

with the ability to cross coral reefs and other submerged obstacles, it had a distinct advantage over conventional landing craft. The drawback was that they were slower at sea and could carry fewer personnel than the LCVP, but nevertheless the LVT proved extremely valuable in the Pacific theatre and underwent a number of modifications and upgrades. Later models were built,

such as the LVT(4), and were equipped with a stern ramp to facilitate the discharge of cargo. Variants carried heavy machine-guns and even a 3in (76mm) gun as fire support to assaulting troops. LVTs were first employed at Guadalcanal in 1942 in a purely logistic role but demonstrated their assault potential a year later during operations at Tarawa when conventional landing craft were unable to

RIGHT: Troops from the 6th US Marines practise landing from an LVT in Virginia during World War II. Early LVTs did not have a stern ramp which complicated the process of disembarkation.

148

negotiate the coral reef that encircled the island. Amphibious tractors – or 'amtracs' as they were known – participated in all of the remaining Pacific operations. By the end of the war, the United States had built a total of over 11,000 LVTs.

LVTs continued in service with the USMC and a number of other armed forces after World War II. Postwar US doctrine continued to emphasize the use of amphibious vehicles in assault operations. In Vietnam, the USMC-operated LVTP-5s were able to carry 37 men. Although not as vulnerable ashore as earlier LVTs, the LVTP-5 still lacked the mobility and survivability of a conventional armoured personnel carrier.

This vehicle was eventually replaced by the LVTP-7 and later the LVTP-7A1 (also known as the AAV-7A1). This vehicle has a maximum speed of 8 knots at sea and up to 45mph (72kph) on land; it has proved attractive to many foregin navies and has been exported to Argentina, Brazil, Italy, South Korea, Spain, Thailand and Venezuela. The continued vulnerability of the LVTP-7A1 ashore has led to the development of appliqué armour kits that reduce vulnerability to anti-armour weapons; but, as ever, the need to operate on both land and sea means that this vehicle is not as quick, as safe or as heavily armoured as its single-role counterparts.

ABOVE: A Centurion BARV (Beach Armoured Recovery Vehicle) tows a Land Rover One-Tonne truck during a NATO exercise off the Scottish coast in the 1980s.

BELOW: USS *Wasp*, lead ship of a class of assault ships, which were conceived with a secondary sea-control role. They therefore incorporate maintenance facilities for at least 20 Harriers and up to six ASW helicopters. The flight deck is so long that no ski jump is required.

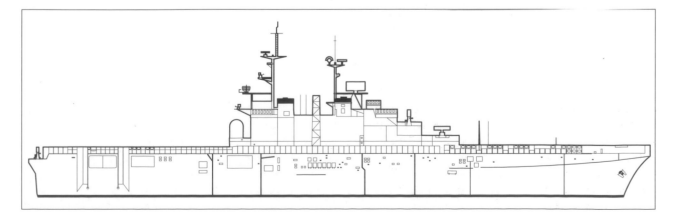

The USMC will shortly accept into service a new amphibious vehicle, to be known as the Advanced Amphibious Assault Vehicle (AAAV). As the name suggests, the AAAV will be a highly advanced vehicle, made from welded aluminium and protected by modular ceramic armour. In order to achieve high speeds at sea, it will use a planning hull, enabling it to achieve speeds of around 25 knots. It is designed to have a road speed of 45mph (72kph). Capable of carrying 18 fully equipped Marines and fitted with an electronically powered turret armed with a 1.2in (30mm) cannon, thermal night-sight and computerized fire control, the AAAV should be a very capable vehicle. If it lives up to all these expectations, it may finally overcome many of the limitations that have afflicted all previous amphibious vehicles.

AIR CUSHION VEHICLES

Air cushion vehicles (ACVs) – otherwise known as hovercraft – have many attributes that make them useful in amphibious operations. They can achieve very high speeds in calm seas. As they travel on a cushion of air above the water's surface, they can operate in waters and across beaches denied to conventional landing craft. The US LCAC can land on 70 per cent of the world's beaches, compared to only 17 per cent for a conventional landing craft. ACVs also have the advantage of being less susceptible to underwater explosions and to conventional sea mines. Able to operate on land and sea, they can cross to the back of the beach before discharging their cargo, avoiding the need for troops and vehicles to wade ashore. However, they also have some limitations: they can be expensive to build and difficult to maintain; they tend to suffer from high fuel consumption and have reduced performance in high-sea states; they are also very noisy and this can compromise tactical surprise. ACVs are also larger than landing craft with the same load capacity, and they therefore take up more space in any ship carrying them.

Although the hovercraft was a British invention, it was the Soviet Union who pioneered the use of ACVs in amphibious operations. They developed numerous large craft, such as the 500 tonne *Pomornik* class, capable of embarking three main battle tanks, in addition to smaller vehicles such as the 87-tonne *Lebed* class which can carry 40 tonnes of cargo and 120 troops, and can be carried in the Russian LPD. In contrast to the US LCAC, the Russian ACVs have a fully enclosed deck and are therefore suitable for carrying infantry.

From the 1980s the USMC became increasingly interested in ACVs. They have sought to harness the speed and range of these vehicles in order to increase the tempo of amphibious operations, and to allow the valuable amphibious ships to remain far offshore but still able to project forces ashore quickly. The US Landing Craft Air Cushion (LCAC) can travel 200 miles (320km) at 40 knots, far faster than any conventional landing craft. It can carry one main battle tank or 60–75 tonnes of equipment and can embark infantry in an emergency, although the open deck makes this an uncomfortable experience due to noise, dust and air turbulence. Three LCACs can be carried in a *Wasp*-class LHD. The USA has sold two LCACs to Japan and one to South Korea. A number of other countries operate ACVs, including Ukraine and Greece, who use ex-Soviet *Pomornik*-class ACVs, and Britain, who operate small *Griffon*-class LCACs, capable of lifting 16 troops each.

MERCHANT SHIPS

Many navies cannot afford specialist shipping, or are unable to provide enough specialist ships to embark the entire landing force. This is true even of

BELOW: A roll-on, roll-off ferry participates in NATO exercises off the coast of Scotland in 1986. STUFT (Ships Taken Up From Trade) may often be required to transport elements of an amphibious force. These ships can provide vital additional lift capabilities but are not as efficient as specialist amphibious shipping. However, many navies conduct exercises with merchant ships in order to practise unloading supplies without the use of conventional port facilities.

relatively sophisticated amphibious organizations such as the combined UK–Netherlands Amphibious Force. In such circumstances, merchant vessels known as Ships Taken Up From Trade (STUFT) are frequently employed. Such vessels, including the cross-Channel ferry *Norland*, the luxury liner *Canberra* and the cargo ship *Atlantic Conveyor* were employed by the British during the Falklands conflict. These ships have both advantages and disadvantages. Passenger ships and cargo vessels can provide a useful addition to specialist lift capabilities. Unfortunately, merchant ships are not designed for war; they lack the self-defence capability and damage-control systems of naval vessels, making them very vulnerable to enemy attack. While sailing off the Falkland Islands, the *Atlantic Conveyor* was sunk by an Exocet missile fired by an Argentine aircraft, taking with it most of the British heavy-lift Chinook helicopters. Some vessels have limited endurance and many have

limited speed when compared to their naval counterparts. Although it is necessary to allow these ships to keep pace, they can slow down an entire task force. In order to operate in the amphibious role, such ships require additional communications equipment, helicopter flight decks, facilities for unloading into landing craft and some defensive weapons. Such ships are not designed to land troops or equipment without port facilities and so the disembarkation process is inevitably longer and more difficult than with purpose-built vessels. As both officers and crew are likely to be unused to combat situations, they may have to be augmented by military personnel.

Despite these limitations, merchant vessels frequently play a vital auxiliary role to the amphibious forces. Transport of large forces over long distances is strategically and economically more efficient than delivery by land or air. Of all equipment transported to the theatre of operations during the 1990–1 Gulf War, 95 per cent went by sea. The United States has created the US Military Sealift Command to provide ocean transportation for defence purposes, and retains three squadrons of Maritime Pre-Positioning Ships forward deployed with sufficient equipment pre-embarked to provide 30 days of combat supplies to a 17,300-strong Marine force. Likewise, the British currently operate two large roll-on, roll-off ferries specifically to provide strategic mobility for their Joint Rapid Reaction Force and to support and supplement their specialist amphibious capability. Such vessels lack the ability to discharge equipment quickly and effectively without port facilities and therefore are unsuitable for use in the first wave of an assault operation. As such, they can never replace the requirement for specialist amphibious ships.

CONCLUSION

In addition to the specialist equipment outlined above, amphibious operations usually require support from a range of assets. These include surface warships – designed to secure sea control and provide air defence – and may include submarines to provide protection from enemy surface vessels or submarines, and to provide a means of covert entry for special forces. Mine counter-measures vessels are required to clear enemy minefields and logistic support ships are necessary to keep the maritime force resupplied. Air superiority is a vital requirement for any amphibious operation. This may be provided by carrier-borne fighters, such as the F-18 Super Hornet, or the FA2 Sea Harrier, or by land-based aircraft such as the Eurofighter.

Aircraft can also provide long-range strikes against land targets, electronic warfare capabilities, strategic intelligence and airborne early warning. Thus, amphibious operations may require a large mix of forces derived from more than one service. Capabilities on this scale are not cheap. Very few navies are in a position to deploy the full range of specialist amphibious equipment outlined above. However, a large number employ some element of these and thus enhance their ability to project power from the sea to the shore.

BELOW: A prototype of the advanced Eurofighter undergoes a test flight. Future amphibious operations will require support from a variety of joint assets drawn from all three services. Aircraft such as the Eurofighter will be required to provide air superiority, maritime assets must provide sea control, and both will be required to support military operations inland.

CHAPTER NINE

THE FUTURE OF AMPHIBIOUS WARFARE

Amphibious forces must develop new techniques and harness new technology to meet the challenges of the future.

Throughout the history of warfare, there has been an ever-changing balance between offensive capabilities and defensive counter-measures. On occasion, this balance has swung decisively in favour of one or other element. For example, for a period during World War I, attacking armies were unable to overcome the tactical advantages of entrenched infantry which were protected by barbed wire and supported by artillery and machine-guns. By 1918 these difficulties could be counteracted by a mixture of new technology and innovative tactics. Amphibious operations have also been subject

LEFT: A USMC Bell AH-1 Cobra attack helicopter. The employment of offensive assets such as attack helicopters, carrier-based ground-attack aircraft, long-range missiles and precision-guided munitions give the modern commander a far greater range of capabilities than was available in the past. The requirement to organize and support this range of expensive and sophisticated weaponry adds to the potential but also to the complexity of the modern amphibious operation.

RIGHT: A Tomahawk land attack cruise missile (TLAM) is fired from the USS *Bunker Hill* during Operation Desert Storm in 1991. TLAM provides a long-range all-weather precision strike capability against static targets. Its deployment on board US surface ships and submarines (and now Royal Navy submarines) dramatically expands the range of targets that can be engaged by a maritime force.

to this dynamic. A combination of factors on both land and sea saw the means and capability to defend a coastline increase dramatically in the early years of the 20th century. This did not make amphibious forces obsolete, but it did require the development of new techniques and new equipment in order to restore the balance. This development was undertaken individually by Japan, Britain and the United States, with varying degrees of success. The challenge of war provided an opportunity to test and improve equipment and doctrine until, by 1943, the amphibious forces of the Allies had a major new strategic capability. The successful landings in Italy,

France, New Guinea, the Philippines, Burma and against a series of Japanese Pacific island strong-points demonstrated that the balance between offence and defence had been restored. Indeed, Allied victories at Normandy (1944), Iwo Jima (1945) and Okinawa (1945) suggested that the balance had shifted in favour of the offence.

After 1945 the development of atomic weapons once again raised doubts about the future of large-scale amphibious operations. The USMC representative at the Bikini Atoll atomic tests in 1946, Lieutenant General Roy S. Geiger, immediately realized the potency of such weapons when used against traditional, concentrated assaults. In response to Geiger's report, the Marine Corps Commandant set up a Special Board to examine the issue, which concluded that old-style amphibious operations would not be possible against a nuclear-armed opponent. By exploiting speed and dispersion, an amphibious task force would still be able to reach its target destination, despite the threat of atomic attack. Once ashore, it would be too close to the enemy to be a target. It was in the intervening stage, when concentrated groups of slow-moving amphibious craft and vehicles converged on a beachhead, that the force would be most vulnerable. The threat posed by atomic weapons caused some commentators, particularly within the US Army, to doubt the viability of amphibious operations. In March 1949 General Omar Bradley, Chairman of the US Joint Chiefs of Staff Committee, told a Congressional Committee that he felt that the atomic bomb precluded the possibility of there ever being the need for another large amphibious landing.

The USMC did not accept this conclusion but sought ways of making the assault phase quicker and less concentrated in order to reduce vulnerability. As a result, they developed the concept of vertical envelopment, where helicopters could be used to add speed, dispersion and flexibility to the assault phase of an operation. In a similar fashion to the Marine Corps' experiments of the 1930s, the USMC developed new equipment and devised new tactics in order to make amphibious operations viable in the new strategic environment. The balance was restored. In addition to this, experience during the Korean War and in numerous later conflicts demonstrated the important role amphibious forces could play in situations where nuclear attack was not anticipated, and showed the valuable part that helicopters could play in such scenarios.

FUTURE THREATS

Modern amphibious forces face a variety of very potent threats on land, on sea and in the air. Many of these threats are traditional and would have been familiar to commanders in 1944 or 1915; others are quite new. The ability to overcome the challenges that these pose will determine the extent to which amphibious forces will remain relevant in the 21st century.

Successful operations still require the control of the sea within the amphibious objective area and during passage to it. This can be denied by enemy surface vessels, by aircraft, by submarines or a combination of all of these. An enterprising opponent may even attempt

BELOW: Conventional diesel-electric type submarines such as this Russian *Kilo*-class boat pose a potent challenge to maritime forces operating in the littorals. Many small navies, including Iran's, now operate submarines, greatly enhancing their ability to defend their coastline against amphibious attack.

to attack opposition ships in their disembarkation port through sabotage or other covert activity. The proliferation of modern weapons and technology means that even small navies can have a sea-denial capability of some significance. Sophisticated anti-ship missiles can be bought 'off the shelf' from a variety of sources. Fast-attack craft armed with sea-skimming anti-ship missiles – such as the French-built Exocet – are widely available and pose a serious threat to any amphibious task force. Submarines are more expensive and more difficult to operate but are becoming more widespread than before. Quiet diesel-electric boats such as the two *Kilo*-class vessels procured from Russia by Iran pose a distinct threat to even the most capable surface ship; this threat may be enhanced if an enemy possesses advanced air-independent propulsion systems. The construction or purchase of nuclear-powered submarines by any potential opponents would further increase their long-range deep-water capabilities. Whether they are strong or relatively weak, enemy maritime assets will need to

RIGHT: The damage caused to the hull of the LPH USS *Tripoli* after it struck an Iraqi mine in the Gulf during Operation Desert Storm in February 1991. Sea mines continue to pose a serious challenge to even the most sophisticated navies. They are often cheap, low-technology weapons that retain the ability to neutralize the largest, most expensive ships. Some modern mines, in contrast, are highly sophisticated and very difficult to clear.

be neutralized before any amphibious operations can take place.

Control of the air remains a vital factor in any amphibious operation. The 1982 Falklands conflict clearly demonstrated the vulnerability of even relatively sophisticated warships to aircraft that are equipped with bombs and missiles. This has reinforced the need for air superiority. Air defence can be provided by a ship's guns and missiles, as well as by land-based or carrier-based aircraft. However, today, navies may have to operate in hostile regions before a formal declaration of war. In such circumstances, it may be difficult to distinguish between the radar signature of potentially hostile attack aircraft and those of neutral or civilian aircraft. The Iraqi missile attack on the USS *Stark* in 1987 and the mistaken shooting down of an Iranian airliner by the USS *Vincennes* in 1988 highlight the dilemma of whether or not to engage apparently threatening targets. It may be difficult to secure air superiority when permission to launch pre-emptive strikes against enemy airfields is not forthcoming. Even with air superiority, no force is ever completely immune from attack; missiles can be fired from fixed or mobile land-based launchers. In 1982 HMS *Glamorgan* was damaged by an Argentine Exocet missile fired from the back of a truck.

One very traditional but extremely potent weapon facing amphibious forces is the mine. Land mines placed on the beach and in the surf zone retain their ability against landing craft, vehicles and personnel. Sea mines have been a feature of maritime operations in the littoral since the mid-19th century and can be a very effective means of neutralizing superior naval power. In 1950, mines laid off the North Korean port of Wonsan delayed the planned amphibious landing there for so long that the town was eventually taken from the land. Over 40 years later, during the 1991 Gulf War, the threat of mines effectively ruled out the possibility of an amphibious landing in Kuwait without the risk of very heavy casualties. The ability of cheap and unsophisticated mines to damage expensive and sophisticated warships was demonstrated when the LPH USS *Tripoli* and the cruiser USS *Princeton* were both badly damaged while operating in the

Gulf. Modern mines can be triggered by contact, pressure and magnetic or acoustic signature. Many are extremely sophisticated and most are difficult to clear; such mines are widely available. Even the possibility that they are present can slow down or halt inshore operations.

Enemy land forces can be a key constraint. Defences on the beach can make an assault difficult, if not impossible. No navy possesses the range of close-support assets used to support the opposed landings of the 1940s. Future amphibious commanders may be compelled to find beaches that are not heavily defended. Rapid counter-attacks by formed enemy units are also a danger, particularly in the early stages of an operation. Not even the USMC can match the armoured strength of a conventional tank division. Even unconventional opponents can pose a threat to a landing force using man-portable surface-to-air missiles – such as the US Stinger – or anti-armour and anti-personnel mines, missiles and guns. The recent proliferation of ballistic missile technology and fears about the potential use of weapons of mass destruction raise further questions about the vulnerability of traditional static amphibious lodgements.

Modern military forces also face a variety of asymmetric threats. Future opponents may not be conventional armed forces. Experience in the 1980s and 1990s suggests that in many conflicts the belligerents may be armed factions, guerrilla organizations or terrorist groups. These groups are likely to have access to many modern weapons systems

ABOVE: An Iraqi mine on the surface during mine clearance operations as part of Operation Desert Storm. Mine clearance is a risky and time-consuming process, but remains one of the vital skills for any maritime force operating in the littorals.

159

ABOVE: The USMC is the largest and most capable amphibious force in the world today and, alongside the amphibious ships of the US Navy, deploys a range and scale of capabilities unmatched by the armed forces of any other nation.

but they may be difficult to distinguish from innocent civilians. Even conventional military forces can develop new ways of fighting, aimed to counter the military superiority of their opponent. Few future opponents will be as foolish or as obliging as Saddam Hussein was when he committed the Iraqi Army to a conventional battle against a technologically superior Western-led Coalition. In future conflict, it may be difficult to distinguish belligerents from non-combatants, and there is likely to be a need to minimize casualties and avoid collateral damage. The terrorist threat may be significant and, in conflicts where no major national interest is at stake, intervening forces may be unable to sustain many casualties before political will collapses and the operation is called off. With the advance in communications technology, the media's portrayal of events may become more important and may further limit the actions that can be

taken by an amphibious commander.

A particular problem for amphibious forces is that they operate in the very challenging area of the littoral region. The presence of land may constrict freedom of movement, restricting offensive and defensive options. Chokepoints and straits can channel an attack, creating predictable lines of approach. Sensors may be degraded by local conditions. The Falklands conflict showed the harmful effect of land mass on some shipborne air-defence radars. Anti-submarine warfare operations are always particularly challenging in shallow water and such water is easily mined. Almost by definition, any ships operating in the littoral are likely to be close to enemy shore-based defences. This facilitates their attack by land-based systems and also reduces warning time. These problems are exacerbated by the fact that a large number of navies operate ships that are designed primarily for use in deep-water, open-ocean warfare, and their systems are therefore not optimized for power projection in the littorals.

OPERATIONAL MANOEUVRE FROM THE SEA

The US Navy and Marine Corps have been in the forefront of moves to make amphibious warfare relevant in the 21st century. The US Navy policy documents 'From the Sea' (1992) and 'Forward... from the Sea' (1994) articulated a shift away from concentrating on open-ocean warfare against the Soviet Union to forward-deployed expeditionary forces tailored to meet the evolving challenges of the post-Cold War era. Amphibious forces play an important part in this strategy. The USMC response was outlined in 1996 with the articulation of a new approach to amphibious warfare, which was called Operational Manoeuvre from the Sea (OMFTS).

OMFTS is characterized as a response to both danger and opportunity, the danger being the unpredictable violence and instability across the globe, characterized by the phrase 'chaos in the littorals', and the opportunity being the recent enhancements in information management, battlefield mobility and the lethality of conventional weapons. Put together, these can be used to increase the potential of sea-based forces to influence events on land directly. OMFTS seeks to exploit the manoeuvre potential of maritime forces to turn enemy coasts into vulnerable flanks, and to provide the means to launch decisive blows against the enemy's vital points. It seeks to shatter enemy cohesion through a series of rapid and unexpected actions, creating a situation beyond the enemy's control. The emphasis is on speed, mobility, deception and surprise, to create confusion, uncertainty and delay in the enemy.

LEFT: US Navy SEALs conduct a search and secure exercise. Special Forces operations are likely to remain important in the future. Although equipped with a range of modern weapons, communications equipment and sensors, modern special forces share the same values of discipline and courage as their pre-decessors of World War II.

RIGHT: A US LCAC is guided in on its final approach to the beach. The LCAC is one of the three key manoeuvre assets that will support the evolving concept of ship-to-objective manoeuvre. The other two are the MV-22 Osprey tilt-rotor aircraft and the Advanced Amphibious Assault Vehicle.

OMFTS exploits the sea as an avenue for friendly movement and a barrier to the enemy. A key part of this approach is the concept of ship-to-objective manoeuvre (STOM). Traditional amphibious operations require a lodgement to be secured ashore into which reinforcements and supplies are built up. The need to secure and maintain this lodgement means that there is an operational pause between the initial assault and the advance inland. Supply dumps in the beachhead give the enemy a focus for counter-attacks and make the landing force significantly vulnerable. STOM seeks to avoid these problems by treating the littoral as a single environment across which landing forces manoeuvre, uninterrupted by topography or hydrography. Forces will not aim to secure a beach, but will thrust inland, straight to their ultimate objective. Command and control, logistics and fire support will all be kept at sea and provided when required, without the need to maintain a lodgement ashore. This increases operational tempo and reduces vulnerability. The overall effect should serve to dislocate enemy forces while maximizing US strengths.

In order to achieve this fully, the USN/USMC plan to make greater use of sea basing. This means that whenever possible, equipment, personnel, support facilities and command and control systems will remain on board ship, rather than be deployed ashore. This reduces the logistic footprint ashore, helping the forces' mobility, increasing the tempo of operations and reducing vulnerability. In part, this new approach is a response to the military challenges faced in inshore operations. To reduce their vulnerability, the US Navy aims to conduct operations from 'over the horizon', projecting power into the littoral danger zone without having to be stationed close offshore.

The USMC argue that a naval expeditionary force based in Spain could fight a campaign on the western side of the Atlantic without having to establish a forward base. The force could pose a simultaneous threat to land at Littoral Penetration Areas (LPAs) at (for example) Richmond, Charleston or Jersey, forcing an opponent to divert his forces to meet all threats. Having decided on a particular LPA, the expeditionary force will identify suitable Littoral Penetration Points (LPPs) through which assaulting Marines will pass on the way to objectives inland. The aim is to exploit the speed and manoeuvre potential of maritime assets and the secrecy provided by 'over the horizon' operations in order to secure operational surprise, and also to secure tactical surprise at the Penetration Point and achieve a decisive effect inland.

Operational manoeuvre from the sea and the related concept of ship-to-objective manoeuvre are dependent on modern technology. Central to both are the triad of manoeuvre assets: the AAAV, the LCAC and the MV-22 Osprey. These should offer the range, speed and payload required to conduct true 'over the horizon' operations. For example, US ships can stay 50nm (92nkm) offshore and still put a wave of loaded LCACs ashore every three hours. This will make them more flexible in the choice of littoral penetration points and less vulnerable to attack. In order to achieve ship-to-objective manoeuvre, the command and control, logistics and fire support must remain sea-based. Sea-basing all of these assets will be very demanding and the concept has yet to be fully proven. Nevertheless, future amphibious ships will be built with this concept in mind and the new US LPD-17 has been specifically designed to facilitate sea-basing.

The employment of new technology may make sea-basing more practicable. Precision-guided munitions will increase accuracy and thus reduce the numbers of shells or missiles required, with a consequent saving in logistic effort. New approaches to the storage and supply of logistics may make sea-basing easier. Extended range munitions and the employment of weapons – such as the Tomahawk cruise missile or the Navy Tactical Missile System – offer the potential for precise long-range fire support from the sea, reducing the need for land-based artillery. Enhancements in information technology and the digitalization and miniaturization of communications equipment may facilitate sea-based command and control. All of these factors should help achieve ship-to-objective manoeuvre. However, some obstacles remain that may hinder the achievement of the USN/USMC vision.

Operational manoeuvre from the sea

and ship-to-objective manoeuvre are dependent on the triad of the AAAV, the MV-22 and the LCAC. Of these only the LCAC is currently in service. Even when the triad is completely operational, some problems may persist. For example, the speed of the MV-22 is one of its greatest assets. Assaulting helicopters are currently escorted by Cobra attack helicopters but the Cobra will not be able to match the speed of the Osprey and thus new methods of escorting these aircraft will have to be found. Alternative means might be AV-8B Harrier jets or the advanced Joint Strike Fighter when it enters service. More fundamentally, sea-basing and ship-to-objective manoeuvre will require a high degree of sea control if they are to be effective. If troops ashore rely on floating assets for all of their logistics, fire support and command and control, then they must be certain that these assets will not be sunk or dispersed by enemy action. Experience at

ABOVE: The LCAC can embark and disembark vehicles from ramps at its bow and stern. The extended range and high speed of this craft means that amphibious operations can be launched from over the horizon, enhancing the prospect of tactical surprise and reducing the vulnerability of the amphibious ships to land-based counter-measures.

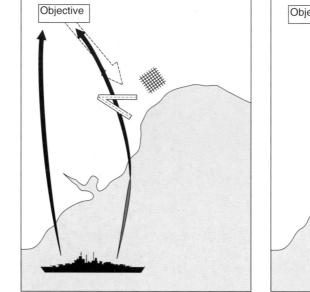

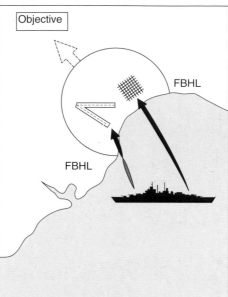

RIGHT: In future (and where possible) the USMC plans to conduct ship-to-objective manoeuvres (seen here on the left) instead of old style ship-to-shore movement (on the right). This is a highly demanding concept, but one that promises to enhance further the value of amphibious forces.

Guadalcanal in 1942 – when the US Navy temporarily lost control of the sea and abandoned the Marines ashore – illustrates the potential problem. The US Navy aspires to gain battlespace dominance in any environment in which it operates, and has specifically chosen to operate over the horizon to reduce its vulnerability to enemy counter-measures. However, war is by nature unpredictable. An enterprising submarine commander might be able to penetrate the protective screen around an amphibious force and attack the vulnerable ships upon which the landing force is totally reliant. Indeed, it is possible that weather might seriously hinder the unloading of supplies. In such circumstances, the absence of supply dumps ashore would prove a weakness, not a strength.

The provision of fire support may be problematic. With the deactivation of the *Iowa*-class battleships, for Naval Surface Fire Support the USMC currently rely on fire from 4.9in (124mm) guns, which have an effective range of only 13nm (24nkm). The new DD-21 Land Attack Destroyer will employ a new 6.2in (155mm) Advanced Naval Gun System, capable of firing extended range munitions to a range of 63nm (116nkm) or more, although the effective range inland will be limited if the firing ship is based up to 50nm (93nkm) offshore. However, both the 4.9in (124mm) and the 6.2in (155mm) shells lack the destructive effect of the battleship's 15.7in (400mm) guns. Long-range guided missiles, attack helicopters and close air support from carrier-based aircraft will provide vital precision fire support, but these do not yet offer the kind of low-cost, high-value, area-suppressive effect of conventional artillery or mortar fire.

There are clearly many challenges facing the successful implementation of operational manoeuvre from the sea; some of these will be solved, others may not be. The USMC is currently involved in an experimental process which seeks to make amphibious forces relevant in a new strategic environment. This was exemplified by the 'Sea Dragon' programme of experiments initiated in 1995 by the Marine Corps Warfighting Laboratory at Quantico. History suggests that they will be successful. Nevertheless, serious questions remain over the relevance of the operational manoeuvre from the sea and ship-to-objective manoeuvre concepts to non-American armed forces, as both concepts rely on large amounts of expensive equipment that may not be available to smaller navies and marine corps. It remains to be seen to what extent other countries will be willing – or able – to adopt these new approaches in future conflicts.

AMPHIBIOUS FORCES OF THE WORLD

Amphibious forces throughout the world vary in their sizes and capabilities. The largest and most capable amphibious force belongs to the USA, with its combined team of the USMC and the

US Navy. The USMC prides itself on its availability and willingness to undertake hazardous duties, revelling in its self-proclaimed label of 'first to fight'. The Marines have traditionally received strong support from the US Congress; in 1952 an Act of Congress mandated that the size of the USMC should not fall below three combat divisions and three air wings. The USMC is currently 171,000 strong and in October 1999 Congress granted it a budget of 11.9 billion dollars for the fiscal year 2000, 1.5 billion dollars more than the Clinton Administration had actually requested.

The primary tactical organization of the USMC is the Marine Air/Ground Task Force (MAGTF). This is a balanced, all-arms force with four functional elements: command and control; ground combat; air combat; and combat service support. There are three main types of these task forces. First, there are the Marine Expeditionary Forces (MEFs),

the principal war-fighting organizations, particularly in times of major crisis. The USMC currently has three of these, each with one division, an air wing and a Force Service Support Group. Second, for lesser contingencies, there are the Marine Expeditionary Units (MEUs), built around a reinforced battalion group and consisting of around 2200 men. This rapid-reaction intervention force is designed and prepared for combat in almost any environment. There are currently seven of these – three based on the east coast and three on the the west coast of the USA, and one based at Okinawa in the Pacific – and they are deployed forward aboard Amphibious Ready Groups (ARGs) in areas of potential crisis, offering the US President a flexible range of military options. Third, Special Purpose MAGTFs are task forces organized for specific purposes, particularly operations such as NEOs and humanitarian support.

ABOVE: A prototype MV-22 Osprey tilt-rotor aircraft carriers a M998 High-Mobility Medium Wheeled Vehicle (HMMWV) slung underneath. The combination of vertical take-off and landing capability and high speed and long range in level flight should make the MV-22 an extremely capable amphibious transport aircraft.

ABOVE: The picture shows the development aircraft DA5, one of two Eurofighter aircraft based at Daimler Benz Aerospace. Aircraft such as the European Eurofighter and the American Joint Strike Fighter will provide sophisticated air defence and strike capabilities. When deployed in support of an amphibious operation they will greatly enhance the maritime forces' overall capability. When they are employed against amphibious forces they are likely to pose a serious challenge.

The US Navy currently has plans to maintain a force of 36 modern amphibious vessels, organized into 12 ARGs. Each ARG is based around a core of three ships – an LHA or LHD, an LPD and an LSD – meaning that, if all of these ships could be maintained in service simultaneously, they would be able to embark 2.5 Marine Expeditionary Brigades. However, serviceability and maintenance routines mean that only around three-quarters of the potential lift is likely to be available at any one time; additional lift will have to be provided by allies or by STUFT. ARGs from the United States and their embarked MEUs have conducted a range of activities in recent years and, in conjunction with the US Navy as a whole, they represent a strong force. Indeed, the integration of naval assets, such as aircraft carriers and surface warships, with amphibious forces has led some US commentators to suggest that the word 'amphibious' should be replaced by the broader term 'expeditionary capabilities'.

The versatility and flexibility of amphibious forces in projecting military power in unforeseen circumstances have prompted a number of European countries to enhance their own forces. The British, French, Spanish, Italians and Dutch have all undertaken programmes to update and improve their amphibious shipping. To this end, the Dutch and the Spanish have collaborated over the design of a new LPD and both navies plan to build two such vessels. In addition, a number of collaborative projects have been undertaken that should increase operational capabilities in the future. The Italian Navy has a relatively sophisticated amphibious force based around three *San Giorgio*-class LPDs with a large new multi-role aviation-capable ship planned for the near future. The Spanish (the Spanish Marine Infantry), Dutch (the Royal Netherlands Marine Corps) and Italians (the San Marco Battalion) all possess small marine forces trained and equipped for amphibious operations.

The largest European amphibious forces are possessed by France and Britain. The French amphibious fleet is designed to support their Rapid Action Force (FAR) and is centred around four LSDs. These will be supplemented by two new LHDs, designed to replace the two *Ouragon*-class ships in around 2005 or 2006. The French Navy has the small commando force of the Fusiliers-Marins to conduct security operations, force protection and special operations. But, the main amphibious force belongs to the Army and is an integral part of the FAR. These troops of the 9th Marine Infantry Division (9 DIMA) practise beach landings and form a highly deployable force that has seen extensive service overseas. They are not specialist Marines in the same sense as the USMC, the British Royal Marines or other dedicated amphibious troops but, nevertheless, the French will soon own a balanced amphibious capability, and the move towards professionalism within their armed forces may allow them to fulfil their full potential in the future.

The British played a leading part in the development of amphibious doctrine and equipment in World War II. After 1945 their amphibious capability has centred upon No.3 Commando Brigade, Royal Marines and the amphibious ships of the Royal Navy. The Royal Navy is currently updating its ageing amphibious fleet, building two new LPDs to supplement HMS *Ocean*, the LPH. In addition, the RFA will shortly receive four 16,000-tonne Alternative Landing Ship, Logistic (ALSLs), and additional roll-on, roll-off ferries have been ordered to provide lift for follow-on forces. The 3 Commando Brigade is an all-arms formation centred around three battalion-sized commando units reinforced with artillery, engineer and logistic support elements. The brigade is supported by its intimate links with the Royal Netherlands Marine Corps, which has been formalized since 1973 in the UK/Netherlands Amphibious Force (UKNLAF). A Royal Netherlands Marine Corps battalion is integrated into 3 Commando Brigade as the fourth

BELOW: Military vehicles are landed directly on to the beach by the British *Sir Bedivere*-class landing ship logistic (LSL), *Sir Percivale*. The British plan to build four new 16,000-tonne alternative LSLs. These ships will not have the ability to beach in the fashion shown here but will land cargo in landing craft from a protected dock in a similar fashion to an LPD or LSD.

manoeuvre unit, and a Dutch colonel is appointed to act as the brigade's deputy commander.

In recent years the British have emphasized the need for joint (inter-service) cooperation and this will mean the integration of army and airforce assets into future expeditionary operations. Most notably, this will include airforce Harrier GR7 ground-attack aircraft and army-operated WAH-64 Apache attack helicopters. The Royal Marines do not operate any armoured vehicles except for their protected all-terrain vehicles; as a result armoured support is routinely provided by light tanks of the Household Cavalry Regiment.

The British maintain close links with the USMC, who appear to value the relationship. Uniquely, USMC units and sub-units have routinely been placed under Royal Marine command. British approaches to amphibious warfare have clearly been influenced by current US doctrine with an increasing emphasis being placed on the possibility of sea-basing and STOM. The British have also begun to talk about the operation of an ARG on similar (albeit much smaller) lines to their US counterparts.

Although the European Union is currently most active on the political and economic level, there have recently been moves to increase cooperation in military matters. In 2000, EU governments pledged to make available enough troops, aircraft and ships to enable a 60,000-strong rapid-reaction force to fulfil a range of missions by 2003. Cooperation and collaboration has been particularly fruitful in the field of amphibious warfare. The UKNLAF was the first significant project and has run successfully for over 25 years. More recently, in 1998 the Spanish-Italian Amphibious Force (SIAF) was established to promote cooperation between these two countries' armed forces. In addition, the activities and capabilities of NATO amphibious forces in the Mediterranean can now be coordinated through the Combined Amphibious Force Mediterranean (CAFMED). In theory, Europe has three brigade-sized landing forces (UKNLAF, SIAF, French), offering the potential for a division-sized lift. Unfortunately, with the exception of the British Royal Marines – who maintain considerable expertise in this field – they currently lack adequate C4ISTAR, sustainability and force integration for full

BELOW: The veteran British LPD, HMS *Fearless* was first commissioned in 1965. It has seen extensive service including action during the 1982 Falklands conflict. After over 35 years of service the ship is tired and worn out. Its sister ship, HMS *Intrepid*, has already been reduced to reserve status and both vessels are due to be replaced by new construction in 2002/2003.

participation in formation-level war-fighting operations. However, continued collaboration in defence matters and the growing interest in amphibious forces may see these difficulties overcome at some time in the future.

During the Cold War the Soviet Union maintained large and powerful amphibious forces but, in common with the rest of its armed forces, the Russian amphibious fleet has declined severely since the break-up of the Soviet Union. On paper they possess a large amphibious fleet, but in reality its power is undermined by old and obsolescent equipment and poorly trained crews. New construction may arrest the decline, although this will depend on the future performance of the Russian economy. Russia retains a Naval Infantry of 14,000 troops organized into one division based at Vladivostok, and three independent brigades based with the Northern, Baltic and Black Sea Fleets.

China is emerging as a major regional power and is committed to increasing its power projection capabilities. Amphibious forces would be of value if the government sought to resolve the dispute with Taiwan through military force, although China probably lacks the numbers and experience to successfully invade Taiwan by sea. Amphibious capabilities may also be of value in the long-running quarrels over ownership of the disputed islands in the South China Sea. China maintains a 5000-strong Naval Infantry Brigade and currently operates 17 LSTs. The Naval Infantry force can expand to eight divisions on mobilization and, in addition, two independent tank regiments and three army divisions have an amphibious role. With enormous economic and military potential, China may become a major amphibious power in the 21st century.

Many other countries maintain an amphibious force of some sort or another. In Thailand the Royal Thai Marine Corps has an amphibious assault battalion and the Thai Navy has recently procured new modern amphibious ships. The Japanese Maritime Self Defence Force has introduced the *Osumi*-class LST which resembles a small LHA in all but name, and the Royal Australia Navy has recently enhanced its amphibious lift. Not all countries aspire to a large amphibious force. That of the Indian Navy is relatively modest given its overall size, and Canada

BELOW: The command ship (LCC) USS *Blue Ridge*. The ship has accommodation for 250 officers and 1300 enlisted men and provides valuable command and control facilities.

ABOVE: Soldiers from the Australian SAS prepare to disembark from an *Oxley*-class submarine in an inflatable boat during an exercise. Covert operations such as these have been conducted since World War II and are likely to remain important in the future.

has no specialist amphibious force. The determining factors are the military and political aspirations of the country in question, so that those countries with a need – or desire – to protect overseas interests and to project military power without using land-based facilities are likely to want amphibious forces. If they have sufficient resources, they may develop them. However, whether or not deployed forces are combat-effective depends on a wide range of factors including training, experience, support from joint assets and appropriate doctrine.

THE FUTURE OF AMPHIBIOUS WARFARE

Previous predictions about the future of amphibious warfare were often flawed. Before World War I and World War II, serious observers claimed that opposed landings would not be possible. They were wrong. In 1949 General Omar Bradley, a veteran of Normandy, stated that he did not believe that major landings would be possible in the nuclear age. Within less than a year, the 1st US Marine Division successfully conducted a major opposed landing at Inchon. In 1981 the British Minister of Defence, John Nott, conducted a major defence review on the basis that the Royal Navy

did not require specialist amphibious ships and that the aircraft carrier HMS *Invincible* should be sold. One year later, these same ships proved vital in the successful campaign to recover the Falkland Islands.

The rapid advance of technology makes predictions about the nature of warfare in the 21st century particularly difficult. By exploiting the potential of new weapons systems – such as unmanned ground and aerial vehicles, long-range precision-guided munitions, efficient cooperative data links and digitized communications equipment, non-lethal weapons, amongst others – future maritime forces may be able to project power in a way undreamt of only a few years ago. New approaches to hull design, such as that employed by the British trimaran research vessel *Triton* or the Australian transport catamaran HMAS *Jervis Bay*, may increase the range, speed or payload of future amphibious ships. The *Jervis Bay* lacks the landing facilities of an amphibious ship, but at 40 knots it, or ships like it, could dramatically reduce the transit time required to reach the amphibious objective area. Low-technology solutions may allow a greater number of nations to develop amphibious capabilities. The

British LPH was built quickly and cheaply using an existing hull design and merchant-navy specifications where possible. Collaborative projects offer another means by which countries can pool their resources and enhance their own forces. The introduction of new ships into the US and other navies may make a number of old, but still capable, second-hand vessels available to those with limited budgets.

Many navies possess a number of amphibious ships in order to support limited transport or logistic activities. Relatively few, however, are capable of landing and sustaining a balanced military force on a potentially hostile shore. The creation and maintenance of such forces is difficult and expensive. Nevertheless, it can also be uniquely rewarding in times of conflict and peace alike.

A well-balanced amphibious force, supported by an appropriate range of maritime and air assets, provides a modern, effective military force ideally suited for the kind of expeditionary operations envisaged in the 21st century. It offers access without the requirement for host-nation support, providing military options that can be translated into political leverage. In situations short of war, an amphibious task force can provide disaster relief, humanitarian support and non-combatant evacuations, and can contribute to peace support operations. In times of conflict, the ability to conduct assaults, raids, diversions and withdrawals has often been the difference between defeat and victory. A modern amphibious force can be balanced, self-sustaining and is capable of manoeuvring at sea and poising offshore for a protracted period without infringing international frontiers.

Amphibious forces are valuable at all levels of conflict and the same force can conduct operations at different ends of the spectrum without the need to reconfigure. They have the ability to exploit the mobility and access provided by the sea and then to land, and support, a self-sustaining military force from a mobile, independent, forward-operating base. This ability has proved to be a unique political and military advantage in the past, and is likely to remain so in the foreseeable future.

BELOW: The *Whidbey Island* class LSD, USS *Gunston Hall*, has been modified to incorporate protection against chemical and biological weapons – a new threat faced by today's modern amphibious forces.. The eight *Whidbey Island*-class ships and the four associated *Harpers Ferry*-class ships are the most modern LSDs in service. They are due to be replaced by the *San Antonio*-class LPDs, the first of which should enter service in 2002.

APPENDIX ONE

Amphibious Ships and Craft

SHIPS

AGF	Amphibious Command Ship
AKA	Attack Cargo Ship
AKF	Ammunition Ship
ALSL	Alternative Landing Ship Logistic
APA	Attack Transport
ATS	Amphibious Transport Ship (Dutch LPD)
ATD	Amphibious Transport, Dock
BTS	Amphibious Transport, Dock (France)
CVHA	Assault Helicopter Carrier (later LPH)
LCC	Amphibious Command Ship
LHA	Amphibious Assault Ship, general purpose
LHD	Amphibious Assault Ship, multi-purpose
LPD	Landing Platform, Dock
LPH	Amphibious Assault Ship, Helicopter
LSC	Landing Ship, Carrier
LSD	Landing Ship, Dock
LSH	Landing Ship, Headquarters
LSI	Landing Ship, Infantry
LSL	Landing Ship, Logistic
LSM	Landing Ship, Medium
LSM(R)	Landing Ship, Medium (Rocket)
LSP	Landing Ship, Personnel
LST	Landing Ship, Tank
LSU	Landing Ship, Utility
LSV	Landing Support Vessel
Ro-Ro	Roll-on, Roll-off
STUFT	Ships Taken Up From Trade
TCD	Landing Ship, Dock (French)

LANDING CRAFT AND AMPHIBIANS

AAAV	Advanced Amphibious Assault Vehicle
AAV	Amphibious Assault Vehicle
ACV	Air Cushion Vehicle
BARV	Beach Armoured Recovery Vehicle
DD	Duplex Drive (amphibious tank)
DUKW	amphibious truck
LCA	Landing Craft, Assault
LCAC	Landing Craft Air Cushion
LCI	Landing Craft, Infantry
LCM	Landing Craft, Mechanised
LCT	Landing Craft, Tank
LCT(G)	landing Craft, Tank (Gun)
LCT(R)	Landing Craft, Tank (Rocket)
LCU	Landing Craft, Utility
LCV	Landing Craft, Vehicle
LCVP	Landing Craft, Vehicle and Personnel
LVT	Landing Vehicle Tracked
LVT(A)	Landing Vehicle Tracked (Armoured)
LVTP	Landing Vehicle Tracked Personnel
MIB	Medium Inflatable Boat
RIB	Rigid Inflatable Boat
RRC	Rigid Raiding Craft

APPENDIX TWO

Abbreviations

ACV	Air Cushion Vehicle
AH	Attack Helicopter
ANZAC	Australia/New Zealand Army Corps
AOA	Amphibious Objective Area
ARG	Amphibious Ready Group
ASW	Anti-Submarine Warfare
ATF	Amphibious Task Force
ATG	Amphibious Task Group
BEF	British Expeditionary Force
CAFMED	Combined Amphibious Force, Mediterranean
CAP	Combat Air Patrol
CATF	Commander Amphibious Task Force
CLF	Commander Landing Force
LPA	Littoral Penetration Area

LPP	Littoral Penetration Point	RNLMC	Royal Netherlands Marine Corps
LPZ	Littoral Penetration Zone	Ro-Ro	Roll-on, Roll-off.
HMAS	His/Her Majesty's Australian Ship	ROE	Rules of Engagement
HMS	His/Her Majesty's Ship	SAS	Special Air Service
MAGTF	Marine Air/Ground Task Force	SBS	Special Boat Service
MAU	Marine Amphibious Unit	SEAL	Sea, Air, Land Special Forces
MEB	Marine Expeditionary Brigade	SIAF	Spanish-Italian Amphibious Force
MEF	Marine Expeditionary Force	SLOC	Sea Lines of Communication
MEU	Marine Expeditionary Unit	SOC	Special Operations Capable
MPS	Maritime Pre-Positioning Ships	STOM	Ship to Objective Manoeuvre
NATO	North Atlantic Treaty Organisation	STOVL	Short Take Off and Vertical Landing
NEO	Non-Combatant Evacuation	STUFT	Ships Taken Up From Trade
NGS	Naval Gunfire Support	TF	Task Force
nm	Nautical Miles	UAV	Unmanned Aerial Vehicle
OECS	Organisation of Eastern Caribbean States	UDT	Underwater Demolition Team
		UKNLAF	UK/Netherlands Amphibious Force
OMFTS	Operational Manoeuvre from the Sea	UN	United Nations
		US	United States of America
PGM	Precision Guided Munitions	USMC	United States Marine Corps
PLUTO	Pipe Line Under The Ocean	USS	United States Ship
RAF	Royal Air Force (British)	UK	United Kingdom of Great Britain and Northern Ireland
RAS	Replenishment at Sea		
RFA	Royal Fleet Auxiliary	VSTOL	Vertical/Short Take Off and Landing

FURTHER READING

Alexander, J. H., *Storm Landings: Epic Amphibious Battles in the Central Pacific* (Annapolis: Naval Institute Press, 1997)

Bartlett, Col M. L., *Assault from the Sea: Essays on the History of Amphibious Warfare* (Naval Institute Press, 1983)

Bartlett, Col M. L. and Alexander, J. H., *Sea Soldiers in the Cold War: Amphibious Warfare 1945-1991* (Naval Institute Press, 1995)

Cresswell, J., *Generals and Admirals: The Story of Amphibious Command* (Longmans, 1952)

Crowl, P. A. and Isley, J. A., *The US Marines and Amphibious War* (Princeton: Princeton University Press, 1951)

Evans, M., *Amphibious Operations: The Projection of Sea Power Ashore* (London: Brasseys, 1990)

Gatchel, T. C., *At the Water's Edge. Defending Against the Modern Amphibious Assault* (Annapolis: Naval Institute Press, 1996)

Lorelli, J. A., *To Foreign Shores: US Amphibious Operations in World War Two* (Annapolis: Naval Institute Press, 1995)

Polmar, N. and Mersky, P., *Amphibious Warfare: An Illustrated History* (Blandford Press, 1988)

Southby-Tailyour, E. (ed.), *Jane's Amphibious Warfare Capabilities* (Coulsdon: Jane's Information Group, 2000)

Thompson, J., *The Royal Marines: from Sea Soldiers to a Special Force* (London: Sidgwick and Jackson, 2000)

Vagts, A., *Landing Operations: Strategy, Psychology, Tactics, Politics, from Antiquity to 1945* (1946)

Whitehouse, A., *Amphibious Operations* (Frederick Muller, 1963)

Jane's Navy International
United States Marine Corps Gazette
United States Naval Institute Proceedings

PICTURE CREDITS
All pictures supplied by **TRH Pictures** and **Chrysalis Picture Library**
except the following: **Mary Evans Picture Library**: 8, 9, 11, 12.